"Jeri Mills' storytelling ability, as well as her deep personal insights, make *Healing is Believing* a captivating look at her journey of discovery into the true nature of healing and energy medicine. The exercises at the end of the book will surely help readers find their own way into that beautiful and fascinating world."
~Barbara Shor, DVM, Interspecies communicator
Author of *Soul of the Wild*

"Jeri Mills is a remarkably innovative physician and healer who is able to balance her conventional medical training and practice with bioenergy medicine approaches. Medicine has been slow to absorb that the physical body can equally be addressed as energy. Dr. Mills brings us the proof that this is so, and opens doors to appreciate that energy is directed and shaped by consciousness."
~Daniel J. Benor, MD
Editor: *International Journal of Healing and Caring*
Author of *Seven Minutes to Natural Pain Release*

"*Healing is Believing* invites us along the courageous journey of one physician who is willing to risk everything in order to find the true source of healing. Her thought provoking and heartfelt stories, along with a generous menu of practical exercises, makes this a must read for those embarking on the path of energy healing, animal communication, or self-discovery."
~Debra Lynne Katz, Author of *You Are Psychic,*
Extraordinary Psychic, and *Freeing the Genie Within.*

(continued)

"The Greek word Holos also means whole. "Holistic" has become widely used to include a comprehensive approach to physical, mental and spiritual health. Indeed the greatest gift we can give to patients is motivation to develop a belief in self and a healthy intention to treat self well. Jeri has given you a sound foundation in *Healing is Believing.*"
~Norm Shealy, MD, Ph.D.
Founding President of the American Holistic Medical Association President, Holos Institutes of Health

"In this ensemble of deeply personal stories, Dr. Jeri Mills inspires readers to enrich their lives by embracing the power of intent and belief."
~Phyllis Winslow, Energy Healer
Graduate of the Barbara Brennan School of Healing

Healing is Believing

a journey into energy healing

Jeri Mills, M.D.

White Sage Press

Readers may contact the publisher at
Jeri Mills MD, PLLC
DBA
White Sage Press
jeri@jerimillsmd.com

This edition was prepared for printing by
Ghost River Images
5350 East Fourth Street
Tucson, Arizona 85711
www.ghostriverimages.com

Cover design by Jeri Mills
Technical graphics by Neil Betrue

ISBN 978-0-9713350-2-8

Library of Congress Control Number: 2013933929

Printed in the United States of America
March 2013
10 9 8 7 6 5 4 3 2 1

In loving memory of
Judie Stoltz and Peter Zorzella

Contents

Acknowledgements

It is with loving gratitude that I salute all the people and animals who have embellished the fabric of my life and have helped to support and guide me through the obstacles Spirit has placed on my path. *Healing is Believing* is as much their story as it is mine.

My heartfelt thanks go to my friends Anita Kindt, Pamela Golden, Jim Pocza, Jeannie Pocza, Sheryal Valencic, Craig Sutter and Karen Rowden who took the time to read the manuscript for *Healing is Believing* and to offer insights that helped me bring this book into its final form. Many thanks also go to my friend and editor Tama White.

I also wish to thank Neil Betrue who helped turn my vision for the cover of *Healing is Believing* into reality, and Mike White for making everything come together.

Namaste.

Holistic healing is more than picking colors from the palettes of both Eastern and Western Medicine and combining them on a single canvas. It's about opening our hearts and our minds to the needs of our patients, being fully present and creating a space where the patient feels safe enough to let go—to heal. When it comes to true healing, the tools we use are secondary to the intention and beliefs that drive our work.

Introduction

How did a physician come to be a Reiki practitioner? For me, energy medicine is the realization of a dream that began when, as a teenager, I started reading science fiction and fantasy novels. Through university, veterinary school and later medical school and residency, whenever I felt frustrated by the limitations of modern society and Western medicine, I escaped to the worlds of Anne McCaffrey and Marion Zimmer Bradley, worlds where people were psychic, where surgeons performed healings with their minds instead of with the crude knives that were the tools of my trade.

It was all just a dream. Then, in 1993, I moved to Tucson, Arizona and discovered real people who were living the life that had always been the core of my dreams and fantasies.

Shortly after arriving in Tucson, I enrolled in a creativity workshop at Pima Community College. The instructor, Diane Ealy, a woman with a PhD in psychology, mentioned in passing that she was able to channel healing energy through her hands. My heart lit up. This bright, educated woman claimed to be able to do what I had always dreamed of.

A few weeks later at a lunch meeting, I asked Diane to tell me more about energy channeling.

"I'm able to draw healing energy from the earth, pull it into my heart and then send it out my hands into other people. It helps them to feel stronger and to heal faster."

"Can anyone do energy channeling?"

"Absolutely."

My heart seemed to beat a bit faster. "Can you teach me?"

"Sure," she replied, but she never did.

Still, the seeds were planted.

Over the next few months, I learned to meditate and developed the habit of sitting and meditating in my car for ten or fifteen minutes each morning before going into the hospital or into my office. I always began the session with one of my favorite exercises from Shakti Gawain's book *Creative Visualizations*. Breathing green, healing energy up from the core of the earth, I let it flow through my body and then allowed it to leave through the top of my head. At the same time, I drew pink, creative energies from the Universe in through the top of my head, let them flow through my body, and then drain out from the base of my spine into the center of the earth.

The sessions left me feeling relaxed and wonderful, but it never occurred to me that I might be able to channel those energies for other people—until there was a need.

One morning when I was working on labor and delivery, the first patient to be admitted to my service was a fifteen-year-old girl in active labor. As I entered the room, she cowered in the back of the bed, arms wrapped protectively around her body. When a contraction hit, she screamed and threw her arms in the air, writhing about the bed like a wild animal caught in a trap.

Until the girl calmed down enough so that we could start an IV, I couldn't give her any pain medicine, let alone the epidural she was begging for.

I did the only thing I could do to help a patient in that situation. I took her hand in mine, looked into her eyes and began showing her how to slow her breathing as we do in meditation or in Lamaze.

Gradually, she started to relax. As we continued to hold hands and take slow, deep breaths, I became aware that I was doing the energy channeling meditation I did in the car every morning, only something was different. Instead of letting the energy run out through the top of my head and the base of my spine, I had been drawing the energy into my heart. I could feel it moving from my heart, down my arm and from my hand into hers.

My patient became calm and still, a poster child for Lamaze! At that point, we did offer her the epidural she had requested earlier. She lay quietly in my arms while the epidural was inserted into her spine and then slept until it was time to deliver her son.

Since that day, I have become a Reiki Master Teacher and have studied Therapeutic Touch, shamanic healing and multiple other healing modalities. I have integrated aspects of all those therapies into the healing work that I offer to friends and patients alike.

Amidst all that study, a very special pattern has emerged: Once I hear that it is possible to do something energetically—anything from opening up the narrow pelvis of a laboring woman to parting the clouds to prevent rain from falling on a special event, even if no one has taken the time to teach me the "necessary techniques"—when the need arises, my body/mind/spirit automatically do what is necessary to perform that healing. There is no conscious effort. I just do it.

For a long time I thought the only limiting factor was my belief that something was possible. Over the years there have been a number of instances where my ego has been shocked to discover that if my patients' belief or will to heal is strong enough, I can be used as the vehicle to bring healing to them to a degree that even I thought was beyond the realm of possibility.

In my first book, *Tapestry of Healing*, I shared the story of my discovery of my own ability to channel energy, and my experiences as I learned more about energy medicine and integrated it into all aspects of my life and my medical practice.

Healing is Believing recalls the next decade of my journey. I have moved from obstetrics and gynecology to the emergency room. I have traveled to many parts of the country, making new friends and saying heart-wrenching goodbyes to others. Through it all I have followed my heart and stepped out of the confines of Western medicine to embrace the world of energy healing, a world where anything is possible, a world where the only limitations are the walls created by my own mind.

The journey has been fraught with lessons about life, about the nature of healing and about myself. The experiences have been uplifting and enlightening, gratifying and humbling. I hope reading about them will bring some of the richness to your life that they have brought to mine.

*The two most important days in your life
are the day you are born
and the day you find out why.*
~Mark Twain

Prologue

Tapestry of Healing had recently been released and the day of my first book signing finally arrived. I had already changed my clothes three times, and my constant pacing across the living room was beginning to make my dogs as jumpy as I was. They all seemed to breathe a sigh of relief when I finally headed out the door.

I spent the first part of the hour-long drive organizing my thoughts and deciding how to start my talk. I figured if I had a good opening line, Spirit would guide me through the rest. When the presentation had taken form in my mind, I turned on a favorite tape and sang along for the rest of the trip, hoping the familiar activity would help me to reclaim my usual calm.

My typical response to stress is a large slice of cheesecake followed by copious amounts of chocolate, but that day the thought of consuming mountains of sweets offered no comfort. So I went shopping.

On my sprint through the mall, I couldn't resist stopping at a cart where a woman was selling angels. I found a wonderful little boy angel holding a puppy, who simply had to come home with me. As I was paying the owner, we started to chat. Bursting with excitement, I couldn't resist telling her about my upcoming signing.

"Oh! You are so blessed to be able to live your dreams!" She smiled and our eyes met in a moment of perfect understanding.

When I was getting ready to leave, the woman went to the other side of the cart, picked up a tiny metal angel and handed it to me. "Here, carry this in your pocket, to bring you good luck."

I finally got to Barnes and Noble, parked the car and hauled in a case of books. When my breath had slowed enough for me to carry on a conversation, I went off to find Lynn, the activity organizer. We relaxed over a cup of tea while she explained how they liked to handle the events at their store, then we walked over to the area where I would give my talk. She started setting up a display of my books while I ran out to the car to get my new jacket.

I had no idea why I had been so compelled to buy the thing, but the moment I slipped into that plum-colored velvet jacket, I was transformed from a nervous writer into a confident author. I took a few slow, deep breaths, said a quick prayer and went back in to join Lynn. By that time, there were already several people waiting to meet me, so I introduced myself and chatted with them till it was time to start.

I began my presentation by describing the events that led me to discover my own ability to channel energy. My audience listened with rapt attention. I could feel their warm acceptance radiating back at me. The knot in my stomach relaxed and I heard a calm, beautifully modulated voice come from my throat. Everything felt right. I was walking my path: healer/teacher/storyteller.

Before our allotted hour was over, I also had time to teach a couple basic self-healing exercises. It warmed my heart to see thirty people sitting on folding chairs in the middle of a busy store, doing guided meditations and making energy balls. As always, I ended my talk with my favorite story from *Tapestry*: The Difference Between Healing and Cure. While my audience wiped away their tears, I answered questions for another ten or fifteen minutes.

Then it was like a dream come true. People lined up with copies of *my* book in their hands. Each person who came to have a book signed stayed for a minute to share some personal story.

One elderly man who had been in a car accident the previous year told me he was still taking narcotics to control the pain. I invited him to sit in a chair and gave him a brief Reiki treatment. When he stood up, he tentatively touched his back. A huge grin lit his face and he said, "I can't believe it! My back doesn't hurt any more."

The story that touched me to the core came from a very small, dark skinned man who had been sitting near the back of the room. He told me he'd been in the store on three different occasions, picked up my book and set it back down.

"I'm glad I came to your talk today," he said. "My friends tell me I can always recognize a true healer and I was drawn to you." I held his hands and we spoke for a few minutes, then he walked away.

A little while later, when most of the crowd had left, he returned and started speaking with me again. "I've been massively depressed since September eleventh. Twenty-five of my friends were killed that day.

"It felt like I received a healing today. I could feel the pain finally release from my body as you spoke to me." With tears in his eyes he continued, "I'm usually not a physical person. It's hard for me to touch other people but...." his voice trailed off.

"Would you like a hug?" I asked.

He smiled.

I stood and held him in my arms for a few minutes. He walked away with a smile on his face. The tears in his eyes mirrored my own. We both received a healing that day.

*Forget not
that the earth delights to feel your bare feet
and the winds long to play with your hair
~Kahlil Gibran*

Desert Magic

There was only one house visible between my little ranch and the distant mountains when we first moved to the desert outside of Sahuarita, Arizona. Miles of mesquite and palo verde trees interspersed with giant sahuaros populated the land as far as the eye could see. It was only an hour drive from the hustle and bustle of Tucson, but I might as well have been in a different world.

I awakened one morning to the unearthly harmonies of a family of coyotes greeting the sunrise. A pair of desert quail, their rolling gait a parody of Charlie Chaplin, waddled across the path, followed by a half dozen chicks barely the size of a hen's egg, but already sporting the characteristic top knot that bobbed on their tiny heads as they twirled in playful circles and then rushed frantically to keep up with their parents. I chuckled at their antics as I strolled down the path to feed the horses.

Early morning chores complete, the dogs and I headed out for a walk. As we approached the ancient sahuaro that graced our yard, the pygmy owl who had taken up residence in a cavity near the top of the giant cactus popped out his kitten-like head. I stopped for a moment and we gazed at each other in silent communion. His morning ritual accomplished, the owl's tiny head disappeared back into the hole. I smiled to myself, thankful for the blessing of having that rare and wonderful creature in my life, knowing that he would be out to greet me again just before sunset.

An hour later I put a bridle on my mare Abbie, and swung lightly onto her bare back. We walked slowly down the dirt roads, winding through the tiny neighborhood that had grown up around us in the four years since our arrival. Children waved at us as their parents tried to herd them into a station wagon, anxious to transport them the two miles to the paved road before the school bus arrived.

A middle-aged woman stood watering the newly planted birds of paradise by her front gate. At our approach, she turned off the hose and came down the driveway to greet us. Abbie extended her neck, always ready for a friendly rub. After a pleasant good morning, the mare and I headed down a quiet path, across an old, dried creek bed.

I began chanting my power song in cadence with the horse's gait as we meandered along the trail our own footsteps had created over the years, and reluctantly headed for home.

Later that morning, the horses munched contentedly on generous piles of hay while the dogs snoozed at their feet, soaking in the sunshine. Breathing my own contented sigh, I let myself out the gate and went to stand at the base of the giant sahuaro that for me represented the ancient spirit of the desert.

I dropped my denim jacket on the ground and lay on top of it face down, my head cradled on my arms, my chest resting comfortably on the soft earth. With each deep breath, I imagined the healing energies of the planet and the ancient secrets of the sahuaro entering my heart. When I exhaled, I sent love and gratitude from my heart back to the earth and into the giant cactus. The sun shone warmly on my back. A gentle breeze occasionally ruffled my hair. My spirit soared, suspended in a timeless peace.

When my heart felt full, I slowly unfolded my body, stood facing the ancient cactus and bowed slightly in reverence before retrieving my jacket and turning toward home.

As I approached the house, I saw a little black snake sunning himself on the flagstone stoop by my back door. A shiver ran up my spine. When a snake crosses my path, he is always a portent of major life changes to come. So far, the changes had always been for the better, but what could be better than this?

You don't have to see the whole staircase
Just take the first step

Animal Communication

The e-mail announced that my friend Heidi would be hosting an animal communication workshop at her ranch in Benson, Arizona. I adore animals, but I had some serious doubts about my ability to do that kind of psychic communication. When I do healing work, I am primarily kinesthetic, that is to say, I feel energy with my hands. I rarely see auras or hear voices, as some other healers do. Doubts aside, it sounded like fun, so I wrote back and had her add me to her list.

The sun shone brightly into the low-walled courtyard behind Heidi's house. A cacophony of birdsong was occasionally subdued when gusts of wind whipped through the trees announcing that spring had arrived in southern Arizona. After we took some time to get acquainted while warming our hands around steaming mugs of hot chocolate, Heidi introduced Diane, the animal communicator who would be leading our workshop.

"You may not realize it, but everyone is psychic

to some degree or other," Diane began. "Animal communication is just one way that you can direct the abilities you already have. We're going to start with a few simple exercises that will show you that you already have psychic abilities."

She had us pair up and try to send thoughts back and forth to each other. We kept it simple, attempting to communicate images of primary colors or numbers, things that could be verified by the person we were working with. The harder I tried, the more dismal was my failure.

Next, we were told to focus on a photograph of one of our partner's pets and try to communicate with the animal. Our primary goal was to get a sense of the animal's name and age, things that could be easily verified. I could get a pretty accurate impression of the animal's personality, but when it came to the details we were supposed to discover, I was a total wash out.

The third exercise involved "talking" with one of the animals hanging out near the courtyard. With little hope of success after my performance so far that morning, I turned my attention to the two Arabian horses who stood grazing on the other side of the fence.

"Open your heart. Send love to the animal. Tell it how beautiful it is," Diane instructed. "Ask permission to speak with it."

Focusing on the gray gelding who was nearer to

me, I didn't seem to be able to connect with him at all. He was much more interested in the tender spring grass than in anything I had to say.

Suddenly, I sensed a feminine voice in the back of my head, "Don't pay any attention to him. I'm the most interesting one here, the most beautiful too!"

It was different from hearing with my ears. Nonetheless, the message was crystal clear. I wasn't sure whether the white mare had actually broken into my attempt to communicate with her companion and started talking to me, or if I was simply enjoying a colorful fantasy.

At the end of the exercise, we shared our experiences. I shrugged and told them about my little daydream.

Heidi burst out laughing, "You have Lana to a T! She's the most self-centered mare on the property."

Was this animal communication? It felt a lot like the times when I interpreted my little dog Joey's body language for visitors. When he looked longingly up at them, his soulful brown eyes fixed on their faces, a gentle wag to his tail, I would tell them, "He's saying *please* pet me. I'm so cute."

I would never have called it "animal communication." I just knew my little dog. And yet that simple practice seemed to be the jumping off point for the skills we were learning that day.

We ended the day in a field that held about ten horses. We would have the opportunity to touch them while honing our communication skills. Diane told us to run our hands over an animal's body and simply be aware of any place that might feel hot or cold.

I was drawn to a big, gangly gelding named Abner. The minute I laid my hands on him, energy began to flow. To me this meant that he was hurting somewhere. I forgot about the "communication" exercises and shifted into healer mode.

I ran my hands lightly over his back and then along his sides, trying to decide where he needed me. When my hands came to rest over his left shoulder, the energy intensified. The instant I started to sense a change in my hands, the horse turned his head toward me and literally wrapped his neck around my body, holding me in place. His back relaxed, his eyelids drooped and his lips twitched, gently massaging my back. I didn't hear any voices, but the message was loud and clear, "Ooh, that's the place, right there. Don't stop!"

Onlookers chuckled as Abner continued to control the situation. After about fifteen minutes, he released me and strolled off to graze.

"I can't believe it. He's not limping!" Heidi said. "That horse has been lame for as long as I've known him."

As we continued to wander around the field, a little sorrel filly caught my attention. I just love babies. That little girl was about a year old and friendly as a puppy, but something was terribly wrong with her.

"That's Marrakesh," Heidi told us. "She had some kind of problem either while she was inside her mother or during delivery. We're not sure which, but she was born with her neck permanently curved toward her right side. Her head often has that jerky motion you're seeing now. I've been doing physical therapy with her every day and she's slowly getting better. We're hoping she'll eventually be normal."

I couldn't resist putting my arms around the filly and, not surprisingly, the energy started to flow. By the time we said goodbye, her neck was a little straighter. I left her with a kiss on the nose and a promise to send energy.

The day after the workshop, it appeared that my mare Abbie, who has chronic arthritis, was having a bad day. I decided to try a little experiment. I used the Reiki symbols to create an energy vortex in the corner of her stall above the feeder. Then I silently explained to Abbie that whenever she's sore, she should stand in that corner and it would make her feel better.

The other two horses rarely went into her stall, even though the only time any of the stalls were closed off from the adjoining arena was when the horses were fed their pellets, so it seemed like a good place to create a healing space for my girl.

When I went out to feed the following morning, I discovered that Jaimie, my two year-old colt, had a hugely swollen right hind leg. It started just above his foot and went all the way to the top of his stifle.

Jaimie was a typical adolescent, constantly annoying the other horses. He often nipped at Abbie and Sara, my Arabian filly. Other times he would charge at the mares, trying to get them to play with him. I assumed he'd finally gone too far and one of the girls had hauled off and kicked him.

He didn't draw much energy when I tried to work on him, but the next morning I noticed an unusual behavior. Jaimie left his breakfast unfinished and went to stand in the corner of Abbie's stall, by her empty feeder.

I didn't think much of it until a few hours later. I was sitting in a stall reading while the horses nibbled on the remnants of their breakfast when I realized that Jaimie was not in either of the two stalls that had hay left in them. He was standing in the corner of Abbie's stall with his butt pressed into the feeder, right under the place where I had set up the energy vortex. His head hung down, his eyelids were partially closed and he was twitching his lips the way he did when I gave him Reiki.

The following morning the swelling was gone. Jaimie was his usual obnoxious self, bolting around the arena and irritating the rest of the herd.

The next time I sent distance healing to Abner, I could feel the energy flowing and had a sense that I was connected to him, when an interesting idea popped into my head. I wondered if I would be able to use distance healing techniques to set up the same kind of energy vortex for him that I had for Abbie.

"Hey, Abner," I said to him. "I know you like the energy I've been sending you. If you show me your favorite place in the pasture, I'll fix it so you can get more energy whenever you want it."

I suddenly had a vision of Abner standing next to one of the yucca plants in the big lower pasture where he lived. I raised my right hand and drew the Reiki master symbol in the air and visualized it gleaming in the sky, just above the place I was seeing in my mind. I then drew the rest of the symbols I would use to attune someone sitting in front of me. My intent was that the symbols would open an energy vortex for Reiki to flow into the spot I was visualizing.

When it felt done, I began sending energy to little Marrakesh. After a few minutes, I had a similar conversation with her. She showed me a place in the upper pasture where she lived, and I used distance healing to create a vortex for her to use as well.

A few days later, I phoned Heidi and asked how my two equine friends were doing.

"Abner's doing great. He's sound for the first time since they started boarding him here. It's the funniest thing though. Whenever I go out to see him, I find him next to the same big yucca plant. He always stands with his head down and his eyes closed, twitching his lips, just like he did when you were working on him."

She continued, "I was planning on driving him to the vet to have his leg x-rayed, but now that he's gone sound, I don't know that it's worth the trouble or the expense."

"How about Marrakesh?"

"She's doing great! Her little neck looks almost normal. She also seems to be spending a lot of time in one area of her pasture, acting just like Abner."

I burst out laughing and told her about the energy vortexes I had set up. I guess they were working!

A few weeks later, during another phone call, I again inquired about Abner and Marrakesh.

"The filly is still doing great, but Abner has gone lame again."

"Is he still using the vortex I set up?"

"Well, no," she told me. "I got some new horses in last week and had to move him to a different pasture in order to make room for them."

"Heidi, you took him away from his healing place!"

Not long after that, I had my most powerful experience in animal communication. I had just started the eighteen-mile drive from my ranch to the office when my cell phone rang. I was surprised to hear my usually cheerful friend Michal sobbing.

"What's wrong, Mike?"

"It's Isis, my favorite mare." She sighed. "Gary and I were gone last week. When we got home, the girl who feeds the horses told me that Isis had been limping for a few days.

"I rushed out to see her. Her left hock was hot and swollen. She could barely walk. She was hobbling around on three feet just lightly touching her left hind foot to the ground every once in a while, to keep from falling. After applying a warm compress, I called the vet.

"He came out right away and removed a five inch long mesquite thorn from her joint. When he saw how bad it was, he suggested that it might be best to put Isis down and end her suffering. Jeri, I just couldn't do that. I love her. We have to try to get her well."

She sniffled, "So, anyhow, the vet gave her an antibiotic injection, left me a couple more days worth of oral antibiotics and told me to keep applying the hot packs. He said he'd be back in three days to see how she's doing."

My heart ached for her. Injured and infected joints in horses often mean permanent disability or death. The likelihood of successfully treating an infected joint in an equine is slim even with surgical drainage and days of intravenous antibiotics. I doubted there was any chance that some pills and a few hot packs would save Isis. I felt certain the vet's intent was to give my friend time to accept the fact that Isis was suffering, and that the kindest option was euthanasia.

I offered to send energy, hoping to ease the mare's agony until Michal came to the conclusion that putting the horse out of her misery was the best solution. I never imagined that Isis could be sound again.

As I continued to drive down the long stretch of desert road, I held the steering wheel in my left hand, lifted my right and drew the Reiki distance healing symbols in the air while thinking of Isis. When the energy began to flow and I felt connected to the mare, I decided to try out my animal communication skills with this mare I had never met in person.

"Isis," I called out. "If you like the energy I'm sending you, show me your favorite place in the pasture, and I'll fix it so you can get more energy any time you want it, so you can heal."

Suddenly tears were streaming down my face. I was filled with a sense of overwhelming hopelessness that seemed to be coming from the horse. "Isis, Michal loves you. Please try to get well. She'll be heartbroken if you leave her."

The sadness lifted as abruptly as it had arrived.

My mind filled with the image of a white mare standing next to a large mesquite tree. Though I had never visited my friend's ranch or even seen a photo of Isis, I knew the mare was showing me an image of herself standing in her special place.

Keeping that picture in my head, I raised my right hand and drew the Reiki symbols while visualizing them opening up a healing vortex by the mesquite tree.

So there I was, cruising down the highway, praying the policeman who often set speed traps on that road wouldn't pull me over if he saw me driving by with one hand on the steering wheel and the other hand waving about in the air, while apparently talking to myself like a crazy person. Happily, he must have been off fighting crime on some other deserted road that morning, and I continued to send energy, undisturbed, till I arrived at my office.

I sent Isis a final reminder that she could have Reiki whenever she stood in the spot by the tree. Our mystical interlude at an end, I gathered up my belongings and went in to work.

The following day, I phoned to ask how the mare was doing.

Mike reported, "She's still lame, not as bad as she was yesterday, but she's acting really bizarrely. Every time I go out to the pasture with her medicine, I find Isis standing by the same old mesquite tree. She always has her eyes closed, her head down—and she's twitching her lips like she's talking with someone."

A few days later I had another call from Michal. "Jeri, the vet was out again yesterday to see Isis." I braced myself, waiting to hear the bad news. "He couldn't believe his eyes when he saw her. The swelling was gone and she was putting weight on all four feet. She was sound at a walk, so he had me trot her out—and she was perfectly fine!"

It was a powerful lesson for me. I had never imagined that the horse would get well. I sent her energy hoping to ease her pain. Once her sadness lifted, it seems that her will to heal was infinitely stronger than my belief that her recovery was impossible. Though I may be able to channel energy, it was the intent of the mare that gave the energy its power.

It was several years later before I was finally able to visit Michal's ranch. What an emotional moment when, for the first time, I stood face to face with my old friend Isis! She was a grand old lady, happy and healthy.

*Nothing ever goes away
until it has taught us what we need to know.*
~Pema Chödrön

Don't Neglect the Obvious

During my five years in private practice, I had never taken a real vacation or, for that matter, been away from the animals for more than a few hours at a time. Friends finally convinced me that I deserved to do something special for myself. I decided to go to a writers' retreat outside of Ruidoso, New Mexico. Not only would two of my favorite writing instructors be teaching there, a group of healers from the Sierra Dove Center who I had become acquainted with when they interviewed me for a piece in their magazine would also be at the retreat.

It had been an unusually dry spring in Arizona that year. The plants around my home were brittle and parched. Even the prickly pear cactus had lost their usual plump contours and were beginning to resemble brightly-colored prunes.

As I drove high into the mountains of New Mexico, the energy shifted. Dead, brown earth was replaced by rich, red soil. The sight of horses grazing on emerald green fields surrounded by huge copses of evergreen trees fed a place in my soul I didn't realize was hungry until that moment. Careening down the winding roads, lost in reverie, I imagined the joy my own small herd would find in those grassy fields. *Were we supposed to move here?*

Suddenly, my mare Abbie appeared before me and spoke to me for the first time. Her image was sharp and clear. She liked the land. She missed me. Little Sara, meek and still insecure with humans, showed her face and sent an image of herself grazing contentedly in a lush pasture. Chuckie, my little black and white dog showed up, wagging his tail, ebullient with his usual joy. I asked them if they though this might be a good place for us to live. It felt like they were all shouting a resounding "Yes!" for New Mexico.

A number of us arrived at the retreat center the day before it was scheduled to start, so we could attend a poetry reading in town that evening, then have a little time to relax before the official program began.

After the reading at the local bookstore, we adjourned to a country and western bar for a little fun and bonding. There was lots of laughter as we sat around a candle-lit table in the noisy, smoke-filled room.

A 200-pound leather clad giant in a red bandana danced solo around the floor, blissful in his alcohol induced haze, seemingly unaware of the surrounding humanity. Others stomped and twirled to the cowboy rock that vibrated through the room. We tapped our toes and periodically took to the floor when the music became even more irresistible than the warmth of budding friendships. For the first time in a very long while, I had fun. No obligations. No worries. Just fun.

The following morning, with hours to spare before the retreat would officially begin, I met with Diane, one of the Sierra Dove healers. *What a treat for someone to be working on me!* It seemed I was always taking care of everyone else. Diane helped me to release a lot of the burdens I had been carrying and made me aware of a new spirit guide who had come to work with me.

An ancient female voice reverberated in the base of my skull. "Why don't you bake any more? Why don't you feed yourself? You have been closed and stingy."

I quickly realized she wasn't talking about cooking. She was talking about the earthly act of creating, of nurturing myself.

There was enormous truth in her words. I had been spending too much of my life lately just going through the motions, focused on survival, without the joy or creativity that had always fed my soul. I *had* been starving. It was time to make some changes.

The following days continued to be a revelation. I felt young and joyful in a way I had almost forgotten during the years of struggling to make ends meet in my private practice. Doing energy healing had allowed me to become softer, more feminine, while I was practicing medicine, but it was still an uphill battle to work in a system where I was undoubtedly thought of as different. At the retreat, I felt fully accepted. We wrote. We meditated. We chanted. We played.

I wrote poetry, beautiful, wonderful poetry. Pages of it filled my journal. It wasn't until later when I re-read the pages that I realized just how much magic had been captured in my written words. How different from the Jeri I had come to know. This was a part of myself I had not seen for a long while. Strength and beauty combined together.

What could be more perfect?

The following morning, I woke elated as I had been the night before. When I attempted to roll out of bed, I discovered that even as Spirit sent wonderful gifts, a part of me was afraid to move forward. The fear was so powerful it had manifested in my physical reality. My back was in spasm. I could barely move.

I was still able to write and found great joy at the workshop, but the agony caused by the simple act of lifting myself out of a chair made it much more difficult to interact with the other participants. Even a hug became part pleasure and part torture. The warmth that came from pressing my heart against another was over-shadowed by pain when an arm lightly touched my screaming back.

The loss of freedom of movement made me more introspective. The conference shifted from playtime to a serious examination of my life as it had been over the past few years. I had no doubt that large changes were due if the creativity and healing were to continue to blossom and grow. *Was this the time to take action? Was there still more work for me to do in Arizona?* Walks and dancing were replaced with meditation and prayer as our last day approached.

On the final evening, Gerald, a man who had studied with a Native American shaman, offered to perform a healing on me. With overwhelming gratitude, I led him to my room where we would have a quiet place to work.

We closed the windows to shut out the intruding voices of any passers by. There was no CD player, no music, only Gerald and me, alone in the room.

He asked permission to proceed with the healing and said a prayer of protection. His image seemed to blur as he transformed himself into an open channel. A deep voice that was very different from his own issued from his mouth. It was the voice of an ancient one, a grandfather.

"You have a big spirit." The grandfather laughed.

"Why do you always have to be the best? Why do you so often choose to work from your head instead of from your heart?"

Gerald placed his hands on my head. The voice of the old one receded and I was gone to some other place as time slipped away.

Suddenly I was back in the room. I heard the voice of grandfather one more time, "What do you want?"

From the depths of my soul came the answer, that which I had been longing for my whole life. "I want to be connected to the earth, to Spirit and to community."

The air swelled with a symphony of hundreds of native voices chanting. The sound seemed to be carried on the wind, but there was no wind.

Finally, all was silent. The healing was complete. I thanked Gerald, stood easily, then we left to join the rest of the group.

After a long, pleasant evening with my new friends, I fell into a dreamless sleep, only to wake abruptly at 3 A.M. I tried to get up, but the spasms in my back had returned. It took about ten or fifteen minutes to extract myself from the bed. I hobbled to the bathroom like an arthritic ninety year-old. The pain became so severe I was afraid I'd have to bang on the wall and get someone to help me off the john.

I was finally able to walk my hands up my legs till I could stand on my own. I returned to the bed, laid down and put my hands on my back. The Reiki wouldn't flow. And then it struck me.

"Damn," I said aloud. "I was so concerned with the spiritual that I forgot to ask him to take away the pain!"

I heard laughter. It was the voice of grandfather. Almost instantly, the energy began to flow through my hands and the spasm in my back started to relax. I could move again.

I realized that during the healing I had been so determined to change the rest of my life that I had forgotten what is most important, to live in the moment. And I had learned one more lesson: "Don't neglect the obvious!"

Thank you, Grandfather, for the healing and for the lessons.

*Respond to every call
that excites your spirit.
~Rumi*

Healing Puck

During a quiet time at the writers' retreat, my friend Julia from Sierra Dove offered to let me use a healing instrument they had brought along with them. She said it would help whoever held it to release the effects of trauma from their energy field.

I was extremely skeptical of man-made objects that were supposed to be able to perform some type of healing. A number of my patients had spoken with me about their experiences after they purchased magnets and various other gadgets that promised to relieve pain. It seemed to me that, as often as the devices helped some people, they caused harm to others. Many of the users became anxious and irritable after sleeping on their magnetic mattress pads, suggesting to me that the magnets had actually pulled their energy fields further out of alignment rather than balancing them. My advice to those women had always been the same: throw away the device and go see a real healer or acupuncturist.

With that history, I was hesitant to hold the little round disc Julia was carrying, but I respected her and the powerful work she and her companions had done with me. Reluctantly, I allowed her to place the instrument on my palm. It didn't look like anything special. Shaped like a miniature hockey puck, it was about three inches in diameter and an inch thick. Colorful images that resembled some sort of circuitry were printed on one side. The other side was solid red. It appeared to be made of plastic. I was told it contained herbs and bits of semiprecious metals and stones. There was no way to open it. When I shook it, nothing rattled.

My palm became warm and seemed to vibrate even though the disc remained still and cool in my hand. There was no other sense of energy shifting, but suddenly I felt happy.

After playing with the instrument a few times, always with the same positive results, I decided to bring one home with me.

When I returned to work, I shared the instrument with anyone who wanted to use it. I often did energy work in the office, but there simply wasn't time in a busy medical practice to offer a healing to everyone. I could provide all my patients with the opportunity to use the puck. Those who wanted to use the instrument simply held it in one hand while we talked at the beginning of their appointment. I was curious to see how they'd respond to my new toy.

I offered the puck to my patients, their spouses,

friends, drug reps, people from the lab, even someone who just stopped by to ask directions to another
office. By my fourth day back at work, at least sixty
people had used it and only two had declined.

No one had any negative side effects. Some patients said they didn't feel any different when they
held the instrument. Others seemed to relax and
appeared to be a bit more at ease, something that
doesn't always happen in an Ob-Gyn office.

A few people felt so good after holding the puck
that they came back several times a week to sit in
our waiting room and use it again. Some of them
even brought friends or spouses who wanted to try
it out. There was never any charge. It was simply a
gift I could offer to our little community.

Several people had rather dramatic responses
when they held the instrument. Seconds after I
placed the little disc on the palm of a smiling young
woman who had come to see me for the first time,
she burst into tears and began telling me about a
friend who had recently died. After a few minutes,
she smiled and said, "Wow, I never expected that to
come out today. I'm not sure why, but I feel better
now, lighter. Thank you."

When one of our favorite drug reps, a big, muscular young man, came to deliver some samples, I
offered to let him try the instrument as well. He

took it in his hand. After a few minutes, he started telling us about a car accident he'd been in several years earlier.

"I had been in ICU for weeks and no matter what they did, my left leg wouldn't heal. They even spoke with my mom about possibly needing to amputate.

"At that point, my mother decided it was time to bring in some alternative healers. They worked on me once, then taught us some visualization techniques that we both did every day. As you can see, it worked. I have two good legs."

One day, after a series of really lovely patients had come through the office, Susan, my assistant, walked up to my desk at 4 PM and said, "Well, I guess the good streak had to end. This one is miserable and acts like her face will crack if she smiles."

The woman suffered from depression. She also experienced chronic pain from arthritis and fibromyalgia. She was wearing a tens unit that didn't seem to be doing much good and she was, indeed, quite miserable. She used the puck while I told her a little about it and about some of my experiences with other forms of energy healing. The lines in her face began to relax, her voice softened and she started smiling as we talked.

When she left the office, she still had a lot of physical pain but, emotionally, she seemed to be coping much better. The puck and I had given her hope. Ms. F was even thinking about getting a healing instrument of her own.

I went home on a real high. Everyone who came into my office that day went home feeling better.

She stood in the storm,
and when the wind did not blow her away,
she adjusted her sails.
~ Elizabeth Edwards

Gigi's Wedding

There was an unfamiliar voice on the other end of the phone. "Jeri, it's Gigi. It's been long enough since we were all together like a family. I live in Santa Fe now, and I'm getting married next month. I'd like you to come."

My cousin had been little more than a child the last time I had spoken with her, but her invitation warmed my heart. "I'll be there."

I made the eight-hour drive from Sahuarita to Santa Fe the day before I was expected. Though it was only the last week in June, two weeks before the usual start time for our monsoon season and normally the driest time of the year in the desert, there were enormous lightening bolts on the horizon as I pulled into my hotel.

Thunder vibrated the building and rain pelted the roof and windows for hours after I arrived. If the monsoons were indeed early that year, I hoped it wouldn't affect the wedding. (Monsoon season is the time when there are massive thunderstorms every afternoon, usually from July through September. It's a time when our parched desert turns, almost over night, into a fairyland of blossoming trees and flowers.)

There was a flurry of activity in the house when I arrived the next day. Gigi, my Aunt June and cousin Peggy were busy preparing food for the wedding reception, an elegant sit-down dinner for fifty that was to take place in the spacious walled garden behind Gigi's tiny home.

It was sunny and dry that afternoon when we gathered together for a family dinner. I hoped that meant the previous evening's storm was just a fluke.

The following day I came to the house, as requested, a couple hours before the other wedding guests were supposed to arrive, in order to lend a hand with any last-minute details. To my surprise, my previously laid-back cousin was pacing back and forth across the courtyard, chain smoking. My first self-appointed chore was to sit her down, place my hands by her head and let the Reiki flow. After a few minutes, a huge sigh escaped her lips and her shoulders visibly relaxed.

"Thanks. I feel more like myself again." She smiled and went into the house to get ready for her big event.

No longer able to be useful, I curled up in a wicker chair and surveyed the scene around me. In the middle of a large, flagstone-covered yard was a grassy island. In its center an ancient tree towered above the house and spread her branches protectively over the garden. Flowering plants were scattered along the adobe walls. A wooden trellis adorned with roses would serve as the altar. Much of the rest of the yard was filled with long rows of tables covered with white linen tablecloths set with real china and colorful flower arrangements. This was no back yard barbecue they were planning!

The guests were due to arrive within the hour when dark clouds started rolling in. The air shook with the distant rumble of thunder and an occasional lightening bolt lit up the horizon. It looked like the monsoons really *had* arrived. There was no way all those tables could be transferred to the living room that was already filled to capacity with just a sofa and a few easy chairs.

Sighs of dismay echoed all around me. My memory flashed back to a story I'd heard at a healing workshop a few months earlier. Our teacher told us about the time when he had been scheduled to give an outdoor lecture at a large conference and the weather turned.

"It started to rain," he told us, "and I was afraid my talk would be cancelled." A huge grin split the shaggy beard that grew down to his chest. "So I pulled out the bowie knife I always carry, held the knife, blade up, and cut the clouds the way the shamans taught me. Then I planted the hilt of the knife in the ground. The weather cleared and my lecture was a great success." Though no more details about exactly *how* he made the clouds move had been given, and I had never done anything like that before, I knew that if it could be done, I could do it.

"Quick, someone get me a sharp knife," I called out.

In a flash, a wooden-handled carving knife was placed in my hands. With no protocols to guide me, I simply let my body take over. I grasped the hilt of the knife in my right hand and raised my arms to the sky. Standing on the patch of earth beside the ancient tree, I took several deep breaths. With each breath I drew energy from the Universe in through the top of my head and consciously moved it down my body, around my spine and out through the soles of my feet. I felt larger and larger as the energy filled me. Finally, I drew in an enormous breath and sent the energy up my arms, out the palms of my hands and through the tip of the knife. Slicing the knife through the air, I visualized the clouds splitting apart and moving aside.

A prayer spontaneously came from my lips, "Spirit, please help me to move away these clouds. Hold off the rain and let the sun shine down on this yard and on this marriage." I bent and planted the handle of the knife in the earth near the base of the tree, its blade still pointing up at the clouds.

Suddenly large gusts of wind whipped through my hair and screamed in the branches above my head. "Oh no," I thought. "Did I just anger Mother

Nature?" As abruptly as it had started, the wind quieted. A ray of sunlight broke through the clouds and shone directly into the arbor where the ceremony was going to take place. The clouds slowly receded from above the yard.

It was a magical evening. After a Celtic ceremony in which the minister gave honor to the elements of the four directions, my cousin and her beloved were wed.

I had a wonderful time making new friends and getting to know relatives I had always been fond of but had rarely seen since childhood. The evening also held an unexpected gift, just for me. Several cousins asked me to tell them more about the energy work I do and requested sample treatments. Though I had shared my gift of healing with hundreds of people, that day was the first time anyone from my family had shown a genuine interest in what was my life's work and passion. For the first time in a very long while, I truly felt part of a family.

Though the clouds had wetted the neighbors' yards throughout the evening, my cousin's garden remained a dry haven. When the final guest had gone home, I returned to the base of the tree, removed the knife from its place in the earth and thanked the Universe for parting the clouds and shining her light on Gigi's wedding. As I handed the knife back to my cousin, I felt the first gentle drops of rain land on my face.

*We must be willing to get rid of
the life we've planned,
so as to have the life that is waiting for us.
~Joseph Campbell*

Welcome to New Mexico

Longing for an association with kindred spirits, I was drawn to the community of healers I had connected with at the writers' retreat in Ruidoso, New Mexico. After much soul searching, I sold my medical practice, said tearful goodbyes to my friends and neighbors and left my beloved Sonoran desert. The charming little town nestled in its breathtaking mountain wilderness would become my new home.

New Mexico was magic. Miles of piñon forest surrounded my home. Cattle grazed peacefully on the hillsides and herds of deer passed by my yard, occasionally hopping the fences to drink from our watering trough. A fat porcupine frequently waddled along the side of the trail when the dogs and I took our morning walks.

The neighbors at the top of our dirt road welcomed me into their home like an old friend. I can't help but smile when I recall the afternoons we spent chuckling over the latest antics of their grandchildren and my pets while sipping mugs of herbal tea.

My social life blossomed when they invited me

to join the weekly community potluck. Writers and artists mingled with ranchers and housewives. Something interesting always happened when that colorful crowd got together.

In the past, I had been intimidated by large social gatherings, but I quickly discovered that bringing a dish of my own made me feel like less of an outsider. The easy camaraderie of my new acquaintances made Sunday afternoons a joy. For the first time in my life, I was not only able to relax in social situations, I was able to thrive.

Besides making new friends—and finally having an excuse to try out all the pastry recipes I was longing to create—the potlucks offered the opportunity to introduce energy work to a new community of people who, unlike my friends at Sierra Dove, were not familiar with alternative healing. As always, I began by fixing owies for people and using that time to share a few Reiki stories. How better for a shy woman to find ease in a group of new people than by making them feel better?

As often as I have introduced people to energy medicine, I'm still gratified by how ready most of them are to accept something so totally foreign to them. And so, my mission in life and my personal journey were once again gracefully intertwined.

Not surprisingly, many of the folks I came to know in that rural community were as ardent animal lovers as I am. What did amaze me was the diversity of creatures they had welcomed into their homes.

Besides the herd of Arabian horses that was Cynthia's pride and joy, she had several little donkeys and a camel in her back yard. On my first visit to her place, she led me into a corral to get a closer look at some of her horses.

I was immediately drawn to an elderly chestnut mare. As soon as I laid my hands on her, the Reiki began to flow and she wrapped her neck around my body, holding me in place, and gently nuzzled my back. I returned her embrace, shifting my arms so that one draped over her back while the other curved under her chest, over her heart. We stood that way for a good, long while sharing energy and affection.

When we finally separated, Cynthia was shaking her head. "I can't believe she just did that, she usually hates everyone!"

We continued our tour of the stables. The next animal I met was her camel. I was expecting him to be somewhat aloof like the camels I had grown up with on my father's circus. What I found was a ten-foot tall puppy dog. The big fellow didn't hesitate to come to the fence to greet me, his huge head extended for a scratch and a cuddle. After a few minutes, I laid my hands on his shoulder. His body relaxed as he leaned into me and became an energy magnet. His beautiful long eyelashes drifted down and his sensitive prehensile lips quivered. I had a new friend.

The first time I went to Anne and Paul's house, they introduced me to the skunk they had rescued the previous year. That slow-moving fellow was as wide as he was long and was undeniably the fattest skunk I had ever seen. He was happy to be held by anyone who offered a pet and a snack.

The next time I saw them, Anne was sitting in the yard bottle-feeding a baby skunk they had just rescued. His brother was toddling around at her side waiting for his turn. My heart melted as I watched the tiny creature, already a perfect replica of an adult, with his distinctive white stripe and his fluffy tail curved jauntily over his back. I couldn't resist picking him up.

Anne handed me the other bottle. The little fellow drank his fill and then curled into a ball barely covering the palm of my hand, and fell asleep. The Reiki began to flow and didn't stop till he woke up half an hour later, hopped down and waddled off to play with his brother.

I asked Anne how her new charges were doing when I saw her at the potluck a few weeks later.

She shrugged her shoulders. "It's the strangest thing. The baby you held is mellow and affectionate. His brother is hyper and hates to be handled."

A few minutes later, Paul walked into the room carrying a young skunk who was about twice the size he had been the last time I saw him. Paul was struggling to hang onto the little guy who was wiggling and pushing himself away from the man's chest with his front feet.

"That's the bad one," Anne told me.

"May I hold him?" I reached out and Paul transferred the squirming ball of fur to me. I placed him against my chest and gently covered his back with my hands. The energy began to flow from my palms. He gave a giant sigh, collapsed his little body against me and snuggled in for a nap. He was still relaxed when I handed him back to Paul half an hour later.

The next time I ran into Anne, she greeted me with a huge grin. "Jeri, you're not going to believe it. Ever since you held my little skunk a couple weeks ago, he's been as calm and friendly as his brother. I guess you do have a magic touch!"

Miracle:
A shift in perception from fear
to love, understanding and acceptance.

Rip

It was a Saturday afternoon in late July. Contrary to the myth that summers are cool in the mountains of New Mexico, the temperature had reached ninety-five every day for the last two weeks.

I was curled up in bed, trying to get what little relief the ceiling fan had to offer, lost in the pages of one of my favorite novels, when the phone rang.

"Jeri. How are you?"

The minute I recognized Jaimie's voice, an alarm went off in my head. Jaimie is a horse trainer. That time of year she was so busy she barely had time for food and bathroom breaks, let alone a chat on the phone in the middle of the afternoon.

"Jaimie, what's wrong?"

"Rip's in the hospital."

My mind filled with an image of the gentle man who trimmed my horses' hooves. I'd only known them for six months, but Rip's already weathered face had appeared more drawn and his movements were slower each time I saw him. I would have sworn he was a decade older than the sixty years he claimed to be. The last time he was at my ranch, he stopped to rest an arm over the horse's shoulder and chat for at least ten minutes after trimming each hoof.

Horseshoeing can be a dangerous business. My first thought when I heard he was in the hospital was that, no longer able to move as quickly as he used to, a thousand-pound animal had knocked him down and crushed him.

"My God, what happened?"

"Rip's been feeling awful for about ten months now. He's been so exhausted he can barely drag himself through the days. He lost a bunch of weight and he keeps complaining about belly pain. I tried to get him to see a doctor, but you know how men are! Then, a few days ago, his eyes turned yellow with jaundice and I gave him an ultimatum—go to the doctor or I'd kick him out of the house. He finally listened to me.

"They did some tests at the clinic in town and thought he might have gall stones. So they sent him to the hospital in Alamogordo. When he got there, they did a CAT scan and told him he has a huge tumor in his pancreas."

Her voice became strained, but she managed to maintain her calm. "The doctor is almost certain it's cancer. He says they need to biopsy it to be sure. There's no one there who's skilled enough to do that kind of operation, so we're waiting for a bed to be available at University Hospital in Albuquerque." She started sobbing. "This keeps happening. I made my aunt go for tests, and two weeks later she was dead. Then the same thing happened with my brother."

I felt sick. I'd taken care of several people with pancreatic cancer when I was in medical school and, in the last few years, six acquaintances had been diagnosed with pancreatic cancer. Five died within three months of diagnosis. The sixth hung on valiantly, but she too was gone before the end of a year. Rip and Jaimie were warm, wonderful people. *Why would something so awful have to happen to them?*

"Oh, Jaimie, I'm so sorry. Is there anything I can do? Do you want me to come down and give him Reiki? Are you okay?"

"We're okay right now. They could be ready to ship him to the other hospital any minute, so don't drive here. Just send energy."

I immediately sent distance healing for Rip and Jaimie. Then I went to my computer and wrote a letter to the dozen or so friends who frequently sent healing requests to extended circles of people. I asked them to send distance healing and requested that they put Rip on their healing lists and onto the prayer chains at their churches. My one e-mail should have resulted in several hundred people sending energy and prayers for my friend and his wife.

Rip was admitted to the university hospital on Monday. His operation was scheduled for Wednesday. On Tuesday, I drove up to Albuquerque to visit and offer what support I could.

Rip looked small as he lay in the narrow hospital bed rhythmically gripping the edge of the cotton blanket. The white sheets set off the yellow tinge that had entered his skin since the last time I'd seen him. He smiled when I sat on the edge of the bed and took his hand.

After a brief chat, I offered to perform a healing. Though I didn't express my fears to my friends, the doctor side of my brain was certain that Rip had an incurable disease. My only intent as I laid hands on him was that the energy work would strengthen his body and reduce the physical pain while he recovered from surgery. I also hoped it would help give him the courage to face his death more peacefully. I truly believed there was nothing that could be done to save Rip's life.

The healer in me had the wisdom to keep her opinions to herself.

I laid my hands on his abdomen and became a clear channel of healing and light, allowing Rip to draw what energies he might need through me. When the energy ceased to flow, I lifted my hands from his body and prepared to leave. After hugs and well wishes, I headed for home, promising to continue sending energy throughout the next day.

Jaime said she would phone when the operation was finished.

The following day, about twelve hours after the operation had been scheduled to start, I received the long awaited—dreaded—phone call.

Jaimie sounded exhausted, but there was a brightness in her voice that I hadn't expected. "Jeri, he's fine! I can't believe it and neither could the doctor."

"What exactly did he say, Jaimie?"

"He was shocked when he came out of the operating room. He told me that when he looked inside Rip's belly, he was sure it was full of cancer. He said if it were up to him, he would have simply closed Rip up and sent him home to die in peace. But he had to follow protocols. So he took a bunch of biopsies. He couldn't believe it when the pathologist said there was no cancer, only scar tissue. So he took some more biopsies. They were okay too. Then he just took out Rip's gall bladder. He said he didn't know how it was possible, but apparently Rip is going to be fine."

Surprised but elated, I wished my friends well and sent hugs and energy.

A week later, Rip was still in the hospital, recovering from his extensive scar removal. I drove back to Albuquerque for another visit.

Rip was tired and pale, but he had a big grin on his face when I walked into his room.

"The minute you laid your hands on me and I felt the heat coming into my body, I just knew I was going to be fine. And I am!"

I didn't tell him, but I never thought he would be OK. I still wondered if perhaps, in her stress and her desire for her husband to be well, Jaimie had misunderstood the surgeon when he spoke to her after the operation.

While we were chatting, the surgeon walked into the room for his daily visit. I introduced myself as a family friend and fellow physician and asked him what exactly he had seen in the operating room. With Rip's permission, the surgeon told me his story.

"When I opened him up, thirty years as a cancer surgeon told me in no uncertain terms that I was looking into a belly full of cancer. But sometimes my job is just to follow protocols. So I biopsied some of the tumor in the omentum and sent it off to pathology.

"While I was waiting for the results, we continued to explore Rip's abdomen. I felt masses in his pancreas and in all the surrounding lymph nodes, around the common bile duct and in the adjacent tissues."

He shook his head and continued, "I couldn't believe it when the pathologist phoned and said that all he saw was scar tissue. So I dissected some more and sent down some big, hard, irregular lymph nodes that felt like they were full of tumor. Twenty minutes later, I received another call. Scar tissue. I knew there was cancer in that belly, so I took out all the tissue that felt like tumor. The pathologist said it was all benign.

"Finally I got down to his gall bladder—and it was full of stones. I decided this was the damndest case of gall bladder disease I've seen in thirty years. I plan to write it up for a journal."

It may well be that the mass that looked and felt like metastatic cancer really *was* no more than the most unusual presentation of gall bladder disease that Rip's surgeon had ever seen, but in my heart I believe there is another explanation.

Though there were no "pre-healing" biopsies to confirm or deny my own interpretation of the situation, I believe that Rip *did* have cancer, and that the prayers and energy sent to him were able to transmute the tumor into benign scar tissue.

I was amazed and humbled by the experience. I always knew that if I believed something could be done energetically, it was possible. But in my own arrogance after years of giving Reiki to people who had never heard of it and having their pain go away, I thought that *my* belief was the deciding factor. I saw the patient as little more than a passive recipient.

I have come to understand through this experience that while intent and belief are indeed the driving force behind all healings, the intent and belief of the patient are at least as important as my own.

Clearly, Rip's intent and belief that he would be well, together with the intent and belief of the hundreds of friends and well wishers who sent prayers and energy, were infinitely more powerful than my own belief that it was *not* possible for him to survive his illness. My own importance in the process was demoted to its rightful place. I am merely a vehicle to concentrate healing energy from the Universe. The patient's body, mind, spirit decide what to do with it.

Please understand, I am NOT by any means advocating that if someone believes they will be fine they should forgo medical care. What I do believe, what I have observed over many years as a physician and healer, is that regardless of whether we are talking about alternative healing or surgery, radiation and chemotherapy, the patients who truly *believe* the modality they have chosen will work for them have the best outcomes.

Undoubtedly, the will to live is a very powerful thing, but it is not enough to simply *want* to get well. You must *believe* you are going to get well. And every once in a while, our beliefs are so strong that, like for my friend Rip, miracles happen.

Some changes look negative on the surface,
but you will soon realize
that space is being created in your life
for something new to emerge.
~Eckhart Tolle

Aikido

Sadly, it was not all love and light in my mountain paradise outside of Ruidoso. The land to the far side of my property housed the woman the locals called the Crazy Lady of the County—for good reason.

While unpleasant, her veiled threats and verbal abuse could be ignored, but there were also real physical dangers. She allowed her stallions to run loose, a practice that is illegal in most states.

I couldn't ride my horses outside the fences of my own little ranch. When her aggressive herd was out and about, I was even afraid to walk the dogs. The explosion of firearms coming from her direction frequently spooked my horses when I was riding in my own yard. *Funny how the gunshots only came when I was on horseback!* I was beginning to feel like a victim in my own home.

After a year and a half, tired of living in fear, and also feeling the need to be in a larger community, I started to think about moving. I found my ultimate destination while studying a map: Loveland, Colorado.

What could go wrong when you lived in Love Land?

Spirit must have agreed, because my house sold for the full asking price, five days after I put it on the market.

I gathered up my belongings and, on a beautiful spring day, friends helped me to pack up the U-Haul. I loaded my animals and we set off for Colorado.

Shortly after I arrived in Loveland, my friend Peter, who was both a Reiki master and a martial arts instructor, called. "You've been feeling like a victim long enough, Jeri. It's time for you to get your confidence back. I've done some research and there's an Aikido school only a few miles away from you in Fort Collins. Of all the martial arts, it's the one that focuses the most on energy, so I think you'll like it. And I know it will make you feel strong again."

I signed up right away.

When I arrived for my first class, early as always, the only other person in the room was a stocky man in his forties. He wore the white pajamas of a martial artist, a brown belt proudly displayed around his waist. A bit anxious in that new situation, I started to chat. His curt responses and the absence of eye contact made it abundantly clear that he had no interest in socializing with the chubby little middle-aged woman in stretch pants who had come to learn Aikido.

As more people arrived, I realized there would be a few other newbies, like me, and a large group of more experienced students, all in the same class. Initially the instructor divided us into two groups. While the advanced people started warming up and practicing fighting combinations, we newcomers were sent off to the other side of the room. With a scowl on his face, Mister Brown Belt came with us, at the teacher's request, to begin teaching us basic movements.

We started with stretches. That was okay. I could do that! Then came the choreography, katas, he called them. There was enough jumping and rotating to make me wonder if my knees would survive the evening. *Why I was there?*

As I watched the advanced folks across the room rolling and tumbling over each other, I was pretty annoyed with Peter for talking me into coming to the class at all.

Finally, we started doing the energy-based exercises I had been looking forward to. The entire group gathered in a large circle. For the first exercise, four people at a time would stand just inside the circle. The rest of us were told to focus our energy in our center of gravity (usually around the solar plexus) and walk around the perimeter of the room. As we passed a person in the central area, he would hold out one arm to distract us.

"If you guys are really centered," the instructor told us, "they won't be able to unbalance you or stop you."

When it was my turn to stand on the inside of the circle, I'm afraid I didn't understand that we were not doing any advanced energy exercises just yet.

Mister Brown Belt came charging towards me with his nose in the air and his chest expanded like a rooster on the prowl. In a bit of a panic, I lifted my left arm, muscles relaxed, and took a deep breath. Visualizing rigid steel, I blew it through my arm. A huge "humph" expelled from his chest just before he landed on the ground at my feet.

"Oh my gosh! I'm *so* sorry," I cried. I really did feel terrible. I'm a healer, not a warrior. I didn't want to hurt anyone.

Without making eye contact with me, he picked himself up and continued walking. I noticed that instead of strutting like a Banty rooster, his posture was relaxed and centered.

When I told Peter about it the next day, he laughingly assured me that if the guy had been centered the way he was supposed to be, it never would have happened.

After the circle fiasco, we were divided into groups. Each newcomer would work with several of the more experienced students. We were told to find a partner for the next exercise. One person from each pair would walk across the room while the other grabbed onto his belt or pants and tried to hold him back. First, we were instructed to just walk normally and see what happened. The next time, the "walker" would relax, focus his energy across the room and move from his center.

The other guys laughingly insisted on pairing me with a man who was six-foot-ten. (He was so big I actually asked him how tall he was.) With my hands tucked into his belt and my legs braced, my bare feet skidded across the polished wooden floor as he strode easily across the room.

When it was my turn, he stood behind me holding onto my clothes. Summoning up all my strength, I tried to walk forward. My thigh muscles tightened and my legs quivered, but I couldn't move forward, not even an inch. Testosterone had dominated over the woman who decked Mister Brown Belt. The men were vindicated.

Then it was time to relax and focus my energy. My shoulders softened and my arms hung loosely at my sides. My knees bent slightly. Visualizing myself at the other end of the room, I focused on my solar plexus and projected my energy to the far wall. Everything seemed to blur around me. My hearing became muffled, as if the sounds were coming through water.

"Wow, she's so relaxed," murmured a male voice.

Releasing my breath, I allowed myself to relax even more. Slowly, my legs began to move. It was like gliding through a dense fog. Limbs loose, I walked effortlessly across the room. The huge man who held on to the back of my pants had no choice but to come along with me or to be dragged.

"I can't believe you just did that," the tall man said, obviously impressed.

"Oh, it's no big deal, just energy," our teacher interjected before I could reply. "Come on, guys, lets go over there and practice some fighting exercises while the newcomers stay here and learn how to fall."

I couldn't help but smile.

Feeling a little taller, I headed for home. That night I had been able to effortlessly move a small mountain. With clear intent and unwavering belief, anything was possible.

*When you do things from your soul,
you feel a river of joy within you.*
~Rumi

Reiki in the Park

We had been in Colorado for a few days when I decided it was time for the dogs and me to explore the area around our new home. It had rained the night before and my skin prickled from the damp cold as the boys and I started our walk at 5:30 that morning.

We headed for the park across the street, the Devil's Backbone they called it, after the mountain that forms its western flank. A rolling green face soared up several hundred feet and was topped by red rocks whose rough, irregular pattern of peaks and valleys reminded me more of a group of dinosaurs lined up tip to tail than of a single backbone.

As we turned off the highway onto the short stretch of road that led to the park entrance, a bobcat raced across the road ahead of us and disappeared into a nearby field, obviously chasing his breakfast.

We crossed one runner who was just leaving when we headed up the trailhead and then saw no other humans till we came to the end of the trail on the way home. It was glorious!

As we reached the top of the first rise, I looked up and saw three elk, a cow and two youngsters, about a hundred and fifty feet above us. It was my first encounter with the creature that is my totem on the Native American medicine wheel. They were huge, gangling beasts. The youngsters, probably yearling twins, though one was a bit larger than the other, watched me for a while. The little one nuzzled his companion then lowered his head and started grazing, seemingly unconcerned by my presence.

We walked up to the level of the main trail as they continued nibbling on the tall grass. I stood for a long time watching them, opening my heart and sending love. After a few minutes, mom walked down the hill till she was about fifty feet from me, and we looked at each other. She remained calm and relaxed. After a few minutes, the dogs and I continued on our way.

As we were heading for home, we met a very pregnant woman and her three year old daughter. The dogs played with the little girl while I chatted with her mother.

She gestured to her belly and said, "I'm just trying to get things going. I've been having contractions in fits and starts for days. It's time for this little one to come out!"

My hands heated up. After a brief hesitation, I smiled and said, "Oh, I guess there's a reason we met this morning. I'm both an obstetrician and a

Reiki master. Reiki is a form of hands-on healing. I've often found that my patients have easier, faster labors after a treatment.

"I'd be happy to give you a brief treatment if you're interested. It may help get things going, but the only thing I can promise is that it will cause no harm."

I was a little afraid she'd think I was crazy or feel threatened, but even though she'd never heard of Reiki before, she gratefully accepted.

I laid my hands on her swollen belly as we stood chatting on the sidewalk near the edge of the park. When the flow of energy from my hands had stilled, I wished her a nice baby and said good-bye. I resisted an urge to hug her and had the odd impression that she was having the same thought.

What a lovely way to begin a life in our new home. I was going to love living there!

Sound when stretched is music
Movement when stretched is dance
Mind when stretched is meditation
Life when stretched is celebration
~Ravi Shankar

Dances of Universal Peace

Two weeks before moving to Loveland, I attended a conference where I became friends with a woman from Boulder. The first time we got together in Colorado she took me to a kirtan, a gathering where people came to participate in an Eastern spiritual practice of responsive chanting and prayer. Besides falling in love with that joyful form of devotion, I met several people that evening who would ultimately become some of my closest friends.

One of them introduced me to the Dances of Universal Peace. The Dances stem from timeless traditions that combine movement, song and story to evoke the spiritual essence that is in everyone. Originally based on Sufi practices, the Dances now embrace all religions and cultures. In a typical evening songs are sung in Arabic, Hebrew, English, Hindu, Sanskrit and Native American languages, just to name a few. The focus of the evening is oneness, a celebration of the similarities of all people.

At the last minute, something came up and my friend was unable to go with me the evening I planned to attend my first dance. I was a bit nervous about showing up alone, but ultimately decided to drive to Fort Collins and give it a try.

As soon as I walked into the room, a woman walked up to me, took both my hands in hers, and really looked into my eyes.

"Welcome to Dances of Universal Peace. I'm Grace, one of the leaders. We're always happy to see a new face in our circle."

There was no doubt in my mind that she was completely sincere. My body relaxed and any remaining apprehensions flew away when several more people greeted me as warmly as Grace had.

I sat on one of the few folding chairs that were scattered against the walls and took a moment to look around. Most of the wood floor was clear except for a six-foot diameter round rug in the center of the spacious room. Several different kinds of drums had been set up on the carpet as well as a full-sized harp. A man sat on one edge of the rug, tuning his guitar. A second guitar was propped on a stand near the middle of the carpet. A red-haired woman was busy assembling the parts of her flute.

Brightly colored banners hung from the rafters above the rug and in the corners of the room. They were painted with words in many different scripts, but the message was always the same. Peace.

Finally, it was time to start. We walked barefoot around the circle, some alone, others in groups of two or three, focusing on our breath and on the connection our feet made with the earth. Then we directed each breath in and out of our hearts.

After several minutes, we all joined hands, forming a single circle, and the group recited the opening invocation. "Towards the one, the perfection of love, harmony and beauty, the only being united with all the illuminated souls who form the embodiment of the master, the spirit of guidance."

Each dance was taught before we performed it, so everyone could participate. The steps were simple. The melodies were haunting. The words, regardless of the language and the tradition, carried messages of peace, of oneness, of reverence for the earth and for each other.

Moving around the circle, we not only held hands, we smiled and looked into each other's eyes. I didn't know those people very well. We had only shared a few words at the beginning of the evening, and yet I felt totally accepted.

We were a small group that night, only eighteen or so. When we stood with our arms around each other's shoulders, our toes touched the rug in the center. Our voices rose in celebration and love, and the room swelled to overflowing.

Later, we sat on the floor, leaning into each other, blending our voices in four-part harmony, and it was beautiful. *We were beautiful.*

The final dance included hugs as we moved from partner to partner around the circle. Hearts open, we embraced each other, sharing all, yet demanding nothing.

As I headed for home, I knew that I would return again and again. I had found something wonderful, something I had been searching for, longed for, since I was a child: a sense of shared purpose and COMMUNITY.

Live your life from your heart.
Share from your heart,
and your story will touch and heal people's souls.
~ Melody Beattie

Into the ER

It had been two years since I closed my medical practice. I'd had a fabulous time meeting new people, learning to be part of a community and immersing myself in so many new and exciting spiritual practices. I loved doing healing work, teaching workshops and speaking at hospitals, but the harsh reality was I needed to find some kind of full-time work, and soon, before my savings ran out. There were a lot of mouths to feed in my household, and telling my horses to go on a diet was simply not an option.

I cringed when I recalled the responsibilities of owning my own medical practice, or the hundred-hour workweeks I had endured in a large Ob-Gyn practice, but I loved taking care of people. I missed practicing medicine.

A friend suggested that, with a little more training, I could make the transition to work in the emergency department of small, rural hospitals. I loved the idea. In my first career as a veterinarian I had worked in an animal ER.

The more I thought about it, the more right it felt. So I contacted a company that employs traveling doctors, took the required classes and—after shadowing another physician for several weeks—I began traveling one week a month to work in several small towns in the North Woods of Minnesota.

The medicine was never boring. I treated everyone from newborns to centenarians. My cases bounced between internal medicine, pediatrics, Ob-Gyn, and minor surgery. Many of the hospitals I worked in were so small that besides working in the emergency room, I also saw clinic patients and functioned as the hospitalist.

Now don't start getting a picture in your head of Jeri the ER Doc single-handedly managing the kind of massive traumas you see on television on *Gray's Anatomy*. Rural medicine is not like that. The job of the rural emergency room physician is to treat minor illness, sew up lacerations, splint fractures, and hospitalize patients who require basic care like intravenous fluids and antibiotics.

For more severely ill or injured patients, we function as gatekeepers. We stabilize critically ill patients and get them transferred as quickly as possible to the closest facility that has the appropriate specialists to provide definitive care. Severe traumas, when they are stable enough, are transported from the scene directly to trauma centers by helicopter and rarely see the inside of little rural hospitals.

When I started working in those remote communities, I was a bit nervous about the reception I would receive when I began introducing energy medicine to my patients and staff. But introduce it I did. I was thrilled to discover that they were not only interested, they were excited to learn about and experience energy healing.

My practice started to take on a pattern. I always touch my patients or hold their hand when I first meet them. Whenever I touch someone who is frightened or in pain, healing energy automatically flows from my hands. After taking my patient's history and doing a physical exam, I offered energy healing more openly while we waited for labs to be run or medications to be administered.

"I do this thing called Reiki. It's an ancient healing art like Healing Touch or Therapeutic Touch. I think it will make your headache resolve more quickly. (Or help lower your elevated blood pressure or help to ease your pain...) If you want to see what it's like, I'd be happy to give you a treatment while the nurse is getting your medications from the next room. All I have to do is place my hands near your head. You may feel heat or pressure, or you may feel nothing. The only thing I can guarantee is that it will cause no harm."

Even in those remote parts of the country where many had never before heard of energy healing, no one refused.

Since ER patients are frequently attached to cardiac monitors and blood pressure cuffs that automatically provide readings every few minutes, we were able to obtain some objective information about my patients' responses to Reiki. People often had significant improvement in their vital signs while the nurse was still in the other room getting their medication out of a cabinet. Elevated blood pressure would drop ten or twenty points. Heart rates would stabilize.

Patients with dangerously low blood pressure improved slightly, even before the nurses were finished inserting the intravenous catheters that would allow life saving fluids to run into their veins. If I lifted my hands away from their bodies before there had been time for an adequate amount of fluid to be infused, their pressure would drop again, only to improve when I placed my hands back on them.

Pain began to subside from injured limbs before any medication was injected. Chronic pain patients learned about a method that might allow them to control their own pain without using so many narcotics. Back spasm, the bane of so many people's existence, could often be relieved in minutes instead of the days it would normally take for the anti-inflammatories, muscle relaxers and hot baths with Epsom salts they took at home to take effect.

Western medical treatment always came first, but the opportunities to do hands-on healing and to gain objective information about patients' responses were endless.

Clearly, it was not possible to keep my hands on a patient the whole time they were in the ER, but in some of the tiny rural facilities where I worked there was often only one patient in the emergency department at any given time, so our little studies could be done without interfering with patient care.

Many staff members asked for sample treatments. While they were receiving their mini-healings, I took the opportunity to share stories about my experiences using Reiki with my Ob-Gyn patients in order to give them a more complete picture of what might be accomplished with energy work.

When she heard that Reiki could also be useful in treating ADHD, one nurse immediately asked if I'd be willing to treat her son. That was just the kind of opportunity I had been hoping for.

Shortly after the end of her shift, she returned to the hospital with her little boy so he could have a Reiki treatment.

I was in heaven, earning a living in a way I enjoyed and being able to share my passion and introduce energy medicine in so many different communities.

At my favorite hospital in Minnesota, there were a few giggles and rolled eyes the first time I offered

Reiki to a nurse with a headache, but when it became clear that she was quickly pain free, the rest of the staff lined up for "sample treatments". Even the full-time physicians in that town were open and receptive to what I had to offer. They experienced Reiki treatment themselves and brought their spouses and children for me to work on as well.

At that time, the nursing home patients in that facility lived down a hall that connected with the nurses' station of the main hospital. Several of those elderly residents spent many hours each day in wheelchairs near the hospital nurses' station.

One lady always sat in a chair with a tray attached to the front so she wouldn't fall out. She screamed and yelled for hours at a time, a horrible result of her advanced dementia. The constant screaming was like torture for the other residents and staff. I can only begin to imagine the personal hell that must have existed inside that poor woman's head to put her into such a state for most of her waking hours.

During one of her worst episodes, I placed my hands at her temples and let the energy flow. Within seconds, she closed her eyes and nodded off to sleep. From that day on, whenever I happened to be around during one of her episodes, I would walk behind her, place my hands at her temples, and as abruptly as if someone had turned off a switch, the screaming would stop, her head would fall to her chest and she'd sleep peacefully for several hours.

The greatest turning point at that facility came when we were taking care of Chuck, a gentleman with end stage Parkinson's disease who had been in the hospital for several days.

Early one morning, I was sitting at the nurses' station writing orders and chatting with some of the staff when Chuck was wheeled out of his room. They brought his chair to the nurses' station and set up a small table in front of him so that he could have a change of scenery and a little company while he ate breakfast. His hand shook so badly, he could barely hold the spoon. More food landed on his pajamas than in his mouth, but he resisted the offers of assistance that would have stripped him of the last bit of independence the terrible disease had allowed him.

He looked on with interest as I placed my hands at Mandy's temples to relieve her headache. A slight smile crossed his lips and he said, "I think I can feel that all the way over here."

"Would you like me to come work on you for a little while?"

"Sure."

Once the nurse's pain was gone, I walked around the desk, stood behind Chuck, lifted my hands to his head, and the Reiki began to flow. Several nurses looked on while they drank their morning coffee. It couldn't have been more than a couple minutes later when Mandy exclaimed, "Oh my God! Look at his hands. They stopped shaking."

The energy continued to flow as Chuck, hand still and sure, picked up his spoon and finished eating his breakfast.

I worked on him a couple more times for no more than five or ten minutes each session during my week-long trip. His tremor continued to improve. The physical therapist was thrilled when he became progressively stronger and more coordinated. The day before I flew home, I saw him take a firm hold on his walker and stride down the hall faster than I could walk on my two good legs. It was hard to believe he was the same man we had to lift into a wheel chair only a few days earlier.

When I returned to that facility the following month, Mandy met me at the door with a huge grin on her face. She couldn't even wait till I finished unloading my car to share her news.

"The week after you left, we were at a staff meeting talking about Chuck's amazing progress after you gave him Reiki. After hearing the story, Doctor J told us he thought he could get the hospital to pay for Reiki classes for any of us who are interested!"

Let yourself be silently drawn
By the strange pull of what you really love
It will not lead you astray
-Rumi

A Little Help From a Friend

I was thrilled to be back at my favorite conference, not only as a participant, but as a speaker that year. It was always so much more than an oversized classroom. It was a space where people of like mind and open hearts came together to share an abundance of wisdom, creativity and joy.

I had already seen several familiar faces and was looking forward to renewing old friendships. The receptions were as warm as I had anticipated, but there was a sadness that seemed to shadow so many of their faces. I couldn't imagine what might be wrong and then, at the first morning session, I saw him.

It had been two years since our last meeting and I almost didn't recognize him. My memory of the dapper man in his trademark three-piece suit was shattered by a cruel reality. His previously energetic gait was now slow and unsteady. A pair of faded jeans hung on his gaunt frame. An oversized flannel shirt draped loosely over an abdomen that was distended like a woman's in the last stages of pregnancy.

When we spoke later in the day, I saw the yellow tinge in his eyes.

I didn't know him very well, but my hands heated up and I knew I had to offer assistance. "You look tired. I'd be happy to do a healing for you if you're interested. Maybe it will help."

A sad smile crossed his lips. "Yes. I am tired. I had a liver transplant earlier this year and my body is rejecting it. I'd appreciate having you work on me."

I followed him as he moved slowly up the stairs to his suite.

He seemed a little embarrassed when he said, "The entire lower half of my body is so swollen that it's hard for me to walk. Do you think you can do anything about that?"

"I'll try."

I asked him to lie on his back near one side of the bed with his head at the foot so it would be easier for me to reach him.

After clearing myself and visualizing the silver bubble I always surround myself with when doing a healing, I held my arms about eight inches above his body and began sweeping his energy field from head to toe. That movement allowed me to identify hot spots or irregularities in his energy field, areas that might represent some kind of problem, and to begin to smooth them away. After a time, without giving it any conscious thought, the direction of my movements reversed.

I made small sweeps into his energy field, starting above his feet and moving up his legs and pelvis, all the while visualizing the excess fluid migrating from the swollen tissues into his lymphatics. I saw the fluid draining back into his circulatory system and going to his kidneys where his body could eliminate it.

I had used a similar technique in the past to drain the swelling from the arms of breast cancer patients whose lymph nodes had been removed. I found it to be much more effective than massage or compression devices for relieving lymphedema. Though we were dealing with ascites that day, it seemed like the right thing to do.

After several minutes, that part of the work felt complete. I rested my hands on his distended abdomen and simply allowed the energy to flow. When I raised my eyes, a being who appeared to be made of shimmering light stood before me in the dimly lit room. A feminine voice resonated deep in the base of my skull. "Will you allow me to step into your body to help you?"

Though I had never seen anything like her before, I felt perfectly safe and at peace. "Please do," I said.

She glided behind me and I felt a subtle energy shift as she stepped into my body, seeming to merge herself with me. The flow of energy through my hands intensified.

I remained completely still. I was no more than a funnel allowing the energy to come through me. After a few minutes, I started moving my hands, pushing at an energy block that I sensed.

I heard feminine laughter in the base of my brain and the same, gentle voice asked, "Who's doing this healing? You or I?"

"Sorry," I replied.

I quickly laid my hands back down on his abdomen and stopped interfering. The energies continued to course through me. Time drifted by. It could have been moments or hours later when the flow of energy from my hands decreased and I felt her gently withdraw from my body.

"Thank you," I said.

The only answer was a peaceful silence.

Later that day, I ran into him in the lecture hall. His face seemed a bit brighter, his back less stooped, his movements more steady. "Remember that problem I told you about earlier?" he asked. "It went away."

I smiled back and we went our separate ways.

Judge each day not by the harvest you reap
But by the seeds you plant
~Robert Louis Stevenson

Walk My Talk

Four years earlier, after the writers' retreat in New Mexico, a group of us went to a friend's house to spend one more night together before heading home.

After a lot of playful bantering while we explored the big, elegant home and decided which bedroom each of us would use for the night, I went to my room to rest and meditate before dinner. I stretched out on the bed, took several slow, deep breaths and laid my hands lightly on my abdomen so the Reiki would flow. (I have combined self-healing with meditation for many years. Once I lay down my hands, the energy starts to flow. It takes no conscious effort on my part to keep it going and, for me, the practice creates a deeper meditation.)

I was jolted from my reverie when I became aware of the information coming from my physical senses. My hands rested on a huge, irregular-shaped mass that started in my pelvis and reached almost to my navel.

In that moment there was no "doctor side" to

my brain, only the terror any woman would experience when she discovers a giant tumor in her body. Images of the many patients I had cared for as they succumbed to the horrors of ovarian cancer flooded my brain. After what seemed like an eternity, I was able to slow my breathing and become enough of a physician to gather what information I could about the thing inside of me.

I slowly ran my hands over my lower abdomen, paying attention to details. I was relieved to discover that the mass could be moved in my belly, it wasn't frozen in place like an advanced cancer. Parts of it were hard, like fibroids, but other parts were softer and more worrisome. There was nothing more I could do until I got home, so I took several slow, deep breaths, willed myself to be calm and simply allowed the energy to flow.

Two days later, I got to my office about a half hour before the first patient was due to arrive and ran to the ultrasound machine. I could finally take a look at the mass that was filling my belly. To my enormous relief, I saw several fibroids, a couple of them quite large. For once, I accepted that there are times when one must be a patient, and phoned my own Ob-Gyn to make an appointment.

After examining me, he agreed it was probably a fibroid uterus but, to be safe, he biopsied the lining of my uterus and sent me for an official ultrasound. Thankfully, my ovaries were small and normal. His sonographer did identify five fibroids measuring from three to five centimeters in diameter. When the biopsy came back, it too was benign.

At that time my only symptoms were heavy menses and rather severe cramping for one day a month, things I could live with, so I decided to do nothing medically. I did, however, begin incorporating a technique I had learned at a shamanic workshop into my daily self-healing sessions. As energy flowed from my hands, I visualized the fibroids being burned to a crisp. I then imagined crumbling the balls of incinerated tumors with my hands until they were no more than bits of ash that could be picked up by my circulation and eliminated from my body.

Over the next few years, there were times when the mass seemed smaller and softer, but I knew that if it had gone back to normal, it would be so small I wouldn't be able to feel it at all when I laid my hands on my abdomen. I couldn't understand why my treatments were failing.

Eventually my own Reiki was no longer enough to control the pain, and I began using a new healing instrument made by my friends at the Gentle Wind Project. It was called a pain puck. It looked a lot like the original healing puck, just a fiberglass disc about three inches in diameter and three quarters of an inch thick. I couldn't explain the technology, but it made the pain go away, helped me to stay calm, and didn't have any negative side effects.

After several years, the symptoms had become so severe that they began to control my life. My own Reiki, the puck and the energy sent by friends were no longer enough to control the pain. I tried taking anti-inflammatories even though they upset my stomach, but they didn't help. I refused to take any form of narcotic. I had seen too many patients lose themselves in those drugs for me to be willing to put them into my own body.

It became so severe that for twelve to twenty-four hours each month I lay huddled on the bathroom floor, wracked with pain, screaming and vomiting. When it got to the point where my shifts at work had to be arranged to accommodate the whims of my body, I finally accepted that it was time for Western medicine to take over.

After examining me, the physician didn't even hesitate. He just talked to me about surgical approach and scheduling.

A couple weeks before my operation, I asked my friend Karen, then a second degree Reiki practitioner, if she would be willing to give me Reiki post-operatively as I had always done for my own patients.

"Sure, I'd be happy to."

"Would you like me to give you your third degree attunement? It can be an exchange of energy for helping me."

She grinned. "Sure, but admit it, you just don't want a lowly Reiki II working on you."

I joined in her laughter. "You got me there, but you have been wanting to go on, haven't you?"

"You bet!"

As the day of the surgery approached, I experienced all the same fears as any layperson facing major surgery. It made no difference that I had performed the same operation dozens of times myself, or that I had reassured hundreds of other women.

It wasn't the operation per se that caused me the most anxiety. Besides being a hopeless control freak, ever since my first lecture on the subject in veterinary school, when the professor described anesthesia as "controlled death," I have been terrified of general anesthesia.

My doctor refused to do the operation with the local I had requested. I guess he knew I was hoping to watch what he was doing in a mirror—and would have been quite willing to offer advice, solicited or not.

Karen picked me up at my house the morning of the operation. She burst out laughing when she saw that, besides the few toilet articles and the change of clothes I had been told to pack, my duffle bag was overflowing with copies of my book and reprints of articles I had written about the use of Reiki for

Ob-Gyn and surgery patients.

When she finally stopped laughing enough to speak, she said, "Jeri, for God's sake, you're going to have surgery. You are the *patient*. You are not going there to teach a Reiki class!"

"Karen, I never go into any hospital without educational materials. You never know when there will be a chance to teach!"

She shook her head and followed me out to the car.

They allowed Karen to sit with me until it was time for my operation.

When he came to do his pre-op check, I explained my fears to the anesthesiologist. He decided to give me a type of injectable anesthetic that would only stay in my system for a few minutes after he stopped administering it.

After doing their assessment, the nurses started telling me about the different drugs that would be available for post-operative pain management. I explained to them that besides being a physician, I was also a healer and would be using Reiki for pain control. I made it very clear that I did not want to be given any narcotics after my operation.

When a few of them stopped looking at me like I was some kind of lunatic and actually expressed an interest in what I had to say, I told them about some of my own patients' experiences when I gave them Reiki. Then I handed out some of the articles I had brought. One nurse said she had heard of Reiki before and was actually thinking about taking a class herself. So I reached into my bag and gifted her a copy of *Tapestry of Healing*. She accepted it graciously. I could see Karen cover her mouth with a hand to disguise the grin she could no longer suppress.

As they rolled me into the operating room, I saw two scrub nurses standing behind a long table, efficiently laying out and counting instruments.

"I hope you're wearing powder-free gloves." I called out. "I'm allergic to talc. Did they remember to tell you that I'm allergic to iodine?"

"We know. We've read your chart," one of them reassured me as they rolled their eyes at each other.

I'm sure everyone in the room was more than relieved when the anesthetic drugs were injected a few minutes later and the annoying woman on the gurney could no longer interfere with their work.

The next thing I knew, I was in the recovery room, shivering uncontrollably. The nurse at my side immediately offered, "Let me give you a dose of Fentanyl. It will stop that terrible shaking."

"No. I don't want any narcotics. Please, just get me some warm blankets and I'll be fine."

"I think you'll be better if I give you a shot."

"Absolutely not. I'll be fine. If you could let my friend in here, she'll give me a Reiki treatment and the shaking should go right away."

She finally realized she had come up against a brick wall. Shaking her head and mumbling about what a pain in the a-- it was to take care of doctors, she led my friend into the room.

Karen raised her hands to my temples. I could feel the warmth as Reiki began to flow. Within seconds, the shaking had subsided. She followed my instructions and ran energy across the surgical sites in order to re-attach any energy lines that had been disrupted when knives had cut through my tissues.

By the time I was wheeled to the room where I would spend the night, I was wide-awake and perfectly comfortable.

As soon as she finished introducing herself, the nurse who would be taking care of me for that rest of that shift said, "I see you haven't had any pain medicine yet. Your doctor has ordered morphine or Demerol. Which would you like ?"

"Thanks, but I'm not having any pain. If I do, I'll give myself Reiki or else I'll hold the pain puck I brought along with me."

"What's that"

"Reiki is an ancient hands-on healing art. It helps with relaxation and pain control. It's even been shown to accelerate healing. It's a lot like Healing

Touch or Therapeutic Touch. The big difference is that you can treat yourself. I've used Reiki for years to help control pain for myself as well as for my own labor and surgery patients. I've actually written a book about my experiences as well as a number of articles. Would you like to read some?"

She did a double take. "Sure," she finally replied after a brief hesitation. She was looking at me as if she was dealing with a crazy person, but she accepted the article and walked out of the room.

When she returned, I was holding the puck that I was actually using for pain prevention since I really wasn't having any pain.

"What on earth is that?"

I told her a little about the instrument and asked if she'd like to hold it. She reached out and I placed it in the palm of her right hand.

"Wow, I can sort of feel it vibrate."

I smiled at her. "There are no moving parts. What you're sensing is just energy flowing through your hand.

When she handed it back, she looked a little sheepish. "You know, I've had this nagging headache all afternoon and it's gone now. Do you think that thing actually helped?"

I grinned at her. "Well, it always seems to help me!"

There must have been some gossip at the nurses' station because during the course of the evening, an awful lot of nurses and aides came through my room and most of them were neither checking my vital signs nor administering IV antibiotics. It was like teaching a little Reiki seminar. I shared stories about my experiences using energy work to treat my patients over the past decade. Many of the staff asked to hold the healing instrument their colleague had told them about.

While the night nurse held the puck she said, "Boy, it's a pleasure coming into your room. All the other fresh post-op patients are either puking or crying for more pain medicine, and here you are teaching and making all of us feel better."

I'd been in my room for about six hours when the night nurse finally helped me to sit up at the side of the bed. As I swung around, one of the stitches from my abdomen caught on the gown and pulled a little bit.

"Owie."

She immediately went into nurse mode. "Can you tell me how bad the pain is on a scale from one to ten? Do you want a shot or a pain pill?"

I couldn't help chuckling. "I don't have any pain. When the stitch pulled it felt a little like a paper cut, only not as bad. *I* certainly wouldn't take narcotics for a paper cut. Would you?"

She shook her head and smiled.

I actually followed the rules and rang for an aide to help me the first couple times I got out of bed to walk to the bathroom. It soon became clear that I was neither weak nor dizzy. Hating to bother the staff who was busy taking care of actual sick people, I decided to get up myself the next time. There was music playing on the TV and, without giving it any thought, I started dancing along once I was out of bed.

"*Oops,*" the doctor side of my brain seemed to warn me. "I just had major surgery. I probably shouldn't be doing this." So I stopped dancing and walked sedately to the bathroom.

By morning, I had handed out all the books and articles from my suitcase, and at least eight or ten people had been in my room to chat and try out the pain puck.

My doctor came in to do a final assessment and discharge me. "I hear you've been refusing pain medicine"

"I promise you, I haven't *had* any pain!"

He shook his head as he turned to leave the room.

When Karen came to my house to visit the next day, I was bored and definitely not feeling like an invalid. I did four loads of laundry while we chatted over tea.

Two days later, I was breezing through Safeway. The trip was as much an excuse to get some exercise as to buy more food for my already well-stocked pantry.

By post-op day six, the dogs and I were back in the park for our usual mile and a half walk.

On post-op day nine, I was at Dances of Universal Peace. There was a little discomfort under the waistband of my jeans where the doctor's assistant had accidentally cut my skin earlier that day when she removed my stitches, but, vigilant as I was, I could not find any other discomfort in my body.

I was pleased to know that Reiki controlled post-op pain for me as effectively as it had for my patients, but I was still disappointed that the shamanic techniques I used had failed to dissolve the fibroids—and that the surgery had been necessary at all.

I learned a major lesson when my doctor went over the pathology report with me at my final visit. The seven hundred and fifty gram uterus he removed (normal is seventy-five grams) was, as expected, completely benign. The surprise was that there was no evidence of fibroids. The uterine muscle was, however, filled with adenomyosis, a condition similar to endometriosis only the abnormal tissues invade the uterine muscle instead of the pelvic cavity.

Apparently, the shamanic techniques I used to

get rid of the fibroids had worked. Unfortunately, my medical mind had been so fixated on vaporizing fibroids that I had not allowed the energy to do what it needed to do. I had never simply asked for healing. In my medical arrogance, I made a diagnosis and had limited the energy. Instead of being a healer, I had transformed myself from surgeon to psychic surgeon.

If only the doctor side of my brain had had the good sense to step aside and allow the healer to ask for "this or something better," I might not have ended up on the operating table.

The next time I tell my students to just step out of the way and be a golden funnel when they are performing a healing, I will have to pay attention to my own words!

Don't let fear of striking out hold you back.
~Babe Ruth

Spoon Bending

On a lark, my friend Anita and I decided to go to a spoon bending party one Saturday morning. We drove to Fort Collins, where we joined eight other people who were eagerly waiting for the instructors to arrive.

When our instructors finally walked through the door, Mary, the taller one, stopped to look around the room. She said, "Oh my, this is a small group." Then she set the duffel bag she was carrying onto a long wooden table and began laying out a collection of mismatched silverware.

Finally, she raised her eyes and said, "We usually have twenty or thirty people at our parties. It takes a lot of group energy to make spoon bending possible. Clearly, the energy's not going to come from numbers today."

Shrugging her shoulders, she turned to her partner. "We'll just have to come up with a different plan for today's party."

When we introduced ourselves and shared a little about our backgrounds, we discovered that, unlike the typical group led by these women—people with no previous knowledge of energy work who were just out to learn a fun new party trick—everyone in our class was an experienced healer.

Edie, the other instructor, started to smile. "Okay, people, I have an idea. Let's start off with some energy work. We don't have any massage tables here, but I think you can use these big tables instead."

We cleared the tables, paired up and took turns performing healings on each other. We may not have been bending spoons, but it was a great way to get acquainted. By the time we finished, a collection of strangers had turned into a group of friends.

Finally, the instructors thought we were ready for the main event. We gathered round and they shared stories about the work of Uri Geller, an entertainer who became famous for his spoon bending demonstrations.

Then Mary explained the science of spoon bending. "When energy is conducted into a spot on a molded metal object, it briefly disrupts the bonds in the metal. That area of the metal becomes soft and plastic in consistency for a few seconds. During that time it can be easily bent or twisted into a new shape."

The excitement began to build when Edie talked us through the technique we would use. "Hold the spoon in a narrow spot below the bowl." She demonstrated for us.

"Now, take several deep breaths. With each breath, I want you to imagine that you are inhaling white light. Feel it collect in your head. After the third breath, exhale the white light in a quick puff. Feel it move from your head, down your arm and out through the tips of your fingers into the spoon.

"Then, yell, 'Bend. Bend. Bend.' at the top of your lungs, grasp the ends of the spoon in your hands and bend your spoon. It shouldn't take much pressure at all, but you have to be quick, because after a few seconds the metal will get hard again.

"Before we get started, let's see if we can raise the energy level in this room." She turned a CD player on full blast. The old classic "Shout" vibrated the air. When she started moving to the music, no one could resist joining in. Flinging up our arms and stomping our feet, we twirled around the collection of tables and chairs. Inhibitions flew away as we danced through one song after another till everyone was sweating and winded.

The music stopped and without waiting for our breathing to slow, Edie called out, "Now sit down, everyone. Pick up your spoons and take a few deep breaths of energy. Puff it into the spoons. *Now yell!*"

An ear-splitting chorus of "Bend. Bend. Bend," echoed through the room as we twisted our spoons.

It was frustrating to see that, while my companions were creating great angles and curlicues of their tableware, even after several tries, my best effort produced only a slight irregularity in the handle of mine.

I left the workshop elated after spending the day making new friends, sharing healing and dancing, but sorely disappointed by my own inability to bend a spoon.

Being the stubborn, determined woman that I am, I didn't accept failure. When I got home I went on-line to read more about the science and process of spoon bending. Then I decided to relax for a bit, to let it all sink in.

I curled up on the sofa and turned on the TV. As Spirit would have it, the movie, "The Matrix" was on. Within minutes, I was watching the scene where students sit in a room practicing spoon bending. What struck me about the scene was the relaxation of the young bodies, and the instruction they received to *visualize*.

Now I realize that I was only witnessing a Hollywood version of an event, but it made several things click in my mind. First, I am not a loud person. Group activities where people are all shouting and excited, like sports events, don't make me feel like part of the group, they tend to put me into a state of panic. So yelling at the top of my lungs was probably not the best way for me to learn a new skill. Second, *I had been focusing on the process, not on the intended results.*

After a little deductive reasoning (something that, in all honesty, is rarely involved when I do healing work), I decided that the things that would help *me* to focus the energy needed to bend a spoon were to relax and, as suggested by the film, to *visualize*.

I grasped the neck of one of the inexpensive spoons I had purchased for the class between the thumb and the first two fingers of my right hand. Then I took several deep breaths and pictured an increasingly large energy store coming together in my head. When I "blew" the puff of energy through my fingers, I relaxed my spine while visualizing the metal between my fingers relaxing as well, becoming soft and pliant. I gently grasped the ends of the spoon and, with the effort it would take to bend a strand of limp spaghetti, the neck of the spoon became a triple spiral. Thrilled, I quickly re-shaped three more spoons, finding it to be easier with each try.

In the midst of my excitement, the doctor side of my brain reared her ugly head. Maybe I hadn't learned anything at all. Maybe it was only working because I was using cheap, lightweight silverware. So I grabbed one of the good tablespoons from my kitchen drawer and repeated the process. With the same ease, the larger, heavier spoon became twisted and curled.

Unfortunately, I soon recalled the "by the way" from my instructors at the party. While it is possible to disrupt the bonds created when hot metal was poured into a mold and to change its shape, it is not possible to return said metal to its original molded conformation after it has been altered. The moral to this story: Believe in yourself and don't mess with the good silverware.

A few days later, during a phone conversation with my friend Peter, also a Reiki master teacher, I talked him through the process of spoon bending. Later, he taught his daughter Kathleen. They learned quickly, no group energy necessary. All that was required were intent and belief. At their own little party, they ruined all the family's picnic tableware.

During our original conversation, I told Peter that I thought spoon bending was more than just a parlor trick. I believed it was a way to master a skill that would be useful in healing the human body. We just had to figure out how to apply the technique.

Well... Eighteen months later, I finally figured it out!

I was working in the emergency department of a small rural hospital. There was only one doctor, one or two nurses and a tech working at any given time. We could treat minor problems and stabilize critically ill patients. Any patient who was seriously ill, required specialized care or surgery ultimately needed to be transferred to one of the big hospitals in the city about a hundred and fifty miles away.

One evening in early December when things

were quiet in our department, I did a spoon bending demonstration for some of my staff. The next time I was on call, we had a massive ice storm. All the helicopters and planes were grounded and we could count on it taking at least three or four hours for an ambulance to transport a patient to the city on the slippery roads.

During the storm, a seventeen-year-old boy was brought to our ER after he fell on the ice and fractured and dislocated his ankle. His skin was still intact but both lower leg bones were broken and his foot was turned to the side and back while his knee was pointing forward. The boy's foot was cold and grey from inadequate circulation.

I called the pediatric orthopedic surgeon in the city. He immediately started yelling at me, "You have to put the foot back in place yourself. If we wait three or four hours till he can get here, the boy will lose his foot!"

"How do I do it?" I asked.

"Just pull straight," was his only advice before he slammed down the phone.

My only significant orthopedic experience before that day was when I was a practicing veterinarian. With an unpleasant knot in the pit of my stomach, I recalled spending an hour, and all my strength, struggling to reduce the dislocated hip of a forty-pound dog under general anesthesia. Since that time

I had been completely ortho-phobic.

My back ached whenever I thought about my orthopedic rotations in veterinary school. The endless hours bent over an operating table, my fingers numb from gripping a retractor while some orthopedic resident learned how to use metal and screws to reassemble a broken bone, was an experience I hoped never to repeat. Needless to say, I did not take an orthopedic elective in medical school.

When I started working in the ER, I avoided doing orthopedic procedures whenever possible, certain that I couldn't do them because I simply lacked the physical strength.

Now I don't know if you've seen many orthopedic surgeons yourself, but I am reasonably certain that in order to get into an orthopedic residency program you have to be a former football player, a power lifter or a sumo wrestler. The rare orthopedist (usually a token woman to the program) who was not a football player herself always hires a former linebacker to be her surgical assistant. Then she takes up power lifting as a hobby, just to be safe!

So there's middle-aged, five-foot-two, out-of-shape me—scared to death, imagining playing tug of war with this young man's foot—and losing. Not only had I never fixed a dislocated ankle, I had never even seen another doctor fix one. Knowing that he'd lose his foot if I didn't fix it, I realized that I *had* to fix it—so I just *would*.

The emotional saving grace of the situation was that my staff that night consisted of a six-foot-three, three hundred pound nurse who used to work in a big ER and had seen the procedure done before, a six-foot-two, two hundred and fifty pound ER tech and the six foot tall, body building eighteen year old ward clerk I'd been bending spoons for the previous week. Besides being able to provide muscle in an emergency, I liked and respected all those men and knew that the feeling was mutual. Without a doubt, the next best thing to believing in yourself is having folks around you who trust your abilities.

So with the belief that, somehow, I would manage to fix the foot because I had to, and the reassurance that I had lots of muscle in the room if it came to a tug of war between leg and foot, we set up to do the procedure.

Before we anesthetized the young man, he was in a cold sweat and tears were running down his face. Clearly the narcotic injection he received earlier had done little to control the pain in his ankle.

We injected the drug that would put him to sleep for about five minutes. The linebacker-sized nurse held the young man's leg so his knee was pointing forward. His foot was pointing off to the side and slightly backward.

I held my hands on either side of the boy's heel, about half an inch from his skin, and began running energy while I visualized his foot moving into the correct anatomic position. After a few seconds, I gently placed my hands on his heel, "blew" in a puff of energy, like you do before bending a spoon, and began to apply gentle traction. I had probably put about two grams of pressure on his foot, little more than a feather-light touch, when I felt the bones begin to move. It was as if they had taken on a life of their own as they quickly realigned themselves.

Not more than one or two seconds later, Troy, my muscle man on the knee, cried out, "You did it! It's in."

I looked down at my hands and saw that I was indeed holding a normally aligned foot. We watched for several seconds as the young man's foot turned back to a healthy pink.

A few minutes later, our patient woke up. Through half-closed eyes, he watched us put a splint on his normal-appearing foot. His face lit up with a huge smile and he said, "You know, people are always saying bad things about hospitals and doctors, but you people just fixed my foot. Thank you."

After we were done, I began to wonder if the big, muscular appearance typical of all orthopods was just a front. Maybe these reductions really *were* easy and required only a light touch. After all, those bones had virtually moved back into place on their own, as soon as the boy was relaxed and I gave his foot a gentle nudge.

The thought was interrupted when Troy said, "Boy, I've seen people really struggle trying to fix these ankle dislocations. This one sure went in easily."

I spoke with the orthopedic surgeon three days later. "You did a really good job reducing that ankle," he told me. "I don't know what you were so worried about. I plated and screwed the broken bones together the next morning. Since the bones were already so well aligned, it was an easy surgery. The boy did well and has already been discharged home."

There is no doubt in my mind that intent, belief and the spoon bending exercise played a major role in reducing that young man's fracture. Not only did the energy from my hands help to give the boy's bones a shove in the right direction, the exercise helped me to release any doubts I had about my own abilities, and simply allow the Universe to work through me.

Over the years, I have used the same technique whenever I've had to align the ends of a simple fracture or replace a dislocated joint. I no longer doubt my own abilities, and the spoon bending exercise always works!

Energy Balls

Since the release of my first book, I have had the privilege of meeting healers from all over the country. Many of them have shared tales of their most profound healing experiences with me. My friend Mike Powers told me about an experience he had that beautifully illustrates how intent and belief can turn even a simple exercise into a powerful healing tool.

Mike is a Reiki master and Tai Chi instructor. For many years he has taught a Tai Chi class for cancer patients. In an effort to explain the concept of Chi (life force energy) to his students, he uses an exercise many of us learned in our first-degree Reiki classes. He instructs his patients to move the palms of their hands together and apart until they can feel the energy between them, and then he has them form it into an energy ball or "Tai Chi ball," as he calls it.

Mike began his story, "One day after forming her energy ball, a woman who had just begun treatment for throat cancer asked, "Now what shall I do with it?"

"She caught me off guard," he told me. "In those days, I'd never thought about it being a healing tool. It was a parlor trick, a way of teaching people to feel their own energy, no more.

"Without a lot of thought, I glibly answered, "Why don't you rub it onto the places on your face and neck where you're getting your radiation treatments. It may help to reduce the side effects from the radiation." She obviously believed I knew what I was talking about even though I didn't myself."

"How often should I do that?" she asked.

"Oh, at least five or six times a day."

Mike continued, "She took me at my word and started doing what I had suggested. After that, she never needed to take any of her pain medicine and she never developed the burns and blisters they expected to come with her radiation treatments.

"The doctors couldn't understand what was happening. They were so concerned they began rechecking and recalibrating their equipment to be sure she was really receiving all the radiation she was supposed to get. The machines were all working just fine.

"Finally, she was due to receive her last treatment, a massive blast of radiation. The radiation oncologist told her, "This last treatment is twice as strong as any of your previous treatments. It's going to cause a severe burn, lots of blistering and a lot of pain, but it's necessary if we're going to lick your cancer.""

Mike smiled, "Even the doctors' dire predictions couldn't crush the spirit of that determined 72-year-old. She had complete faith that the energy balls would protect her. So she doubled her use of energy balls and went in for the treatment.

"The doctors couldn't believe the results. She developed what looked like a slight sun burn after the last treatment, but she never developed the severe burn or blisters they had predicted."

Mike continued, "Two years later, the same woman walked into my class one day and said, "Hi. I just wanted to say thank you because you changed my life." She gave me a big hug, turned around and left."

A week after hearing Mike's story, I was asked to go to the home of a man undergoing radiation therapy for head and neck cancer, to give him a Reiki treatment. When I first saw Jim, his sunken cheeks and faded eyes made him appear decades older than his fifty-odd years. His speech was slightly slurred and he kept dozing off in the big lounge chair that seemed to swallow up his bony frame. Unable to eat because of the side effects of his radiation treatments, he was so weak that when he pushed himself out of the chair and began his slow walk to the massage table, I was afraid he'd collapse before he reached the other side of the room.

Jim seemed to enjoy his Reiki treatment, as did the bevy of family cats who insisted on joining him on the table and getting their share of the energy.

When we were through, his color was a bit brighter and he seemed to be more present. Before leaving the house, I told him Mike's story about the lady with throat cancer, and taught him how to make energy balls of his own.

I returned to his home ten days later and found Jim to be a changed man. I sat on the floor and gave Reiki to one of the cats while I watched Jim devour two full bowls of soup. His voice was strong as he reported that, for the last three days, he had felt well enough to drive himself the hundred and twenty miles round trip to receive his radiation treatments.

His voice was even stronger as he argued with his wife about a plumbing job he had agreed to do the following day. She wanted him to stay home and rest. He told her he felt just fine and didn't want to be inconvenienced by his cancer any longer.

I spoke with Jim's wife three weeks after the second Reiki session. Jim had continued to give himself "energy ball treatments" several times a day. His appetite remained good and he had gained five pounds. He was about to complete his radiation therapy and was feeling great.

A few weeks later, I heard from Mike again. He was excited to report that he was involved in the care of a third patient receiving radiation therapy for head and neck cancer. Mike was giving the man weekly Reiki treatments and, as with our other two patients, had taught him to make energy balls and instructed him to apply them to the treatment sites several times a day.

The patient seemed to be tolerating the radiation treatments extremely well. He told Mike that his oncologist confirmed that he was in the five percent of radiation therapy patients with the least amount of side affects.

What started out as a cool healing story has proven to be a valuable tool. With only minutes of instruction, anyone can learn to use this simple technique for self-healing and self-empowerment.

We do not see things as they are.
We see them as we are.
~The Talmud

Compassion

During the winter and spring of 2012, I worked in the emergency department of a tiny community hospital about a hundred miles from home. I just loved working there. Not only did that town have some of the nicest patients I had taken care of in a long while, many of them were interested in integrative medicine. All the patients I offered Reiki already knew what it was and several were even Reiki practitioners themselves.

The staff there was not only capable but warm and welcoming. While less informed about complementary medicine than their patients, they seemed to be open to any information I had to offer. Many of them requested mini-healings and two even expressed an interest in taking a Reiki class. It was a delight to be working in such a positive environment.

About two months after I started working there, I received an e-mail from my boss requesting that I call him. His note read, "Don't worry. It's nothing bad or important, just some minor issues to discuss".

After brief hellos he cut to the chase. "I hear that you've been doing Reiki on your patients. I need to tell you that you're forbidden from doing that sort of thing in my hospital. We're working hard here to establish a reputation for quality, up-to-date medicine in this facility and we think you would damage our image with the community. There are no other problems with your work. You just have to stop doing Reiki."

I believe he thought he was being open minded when he continued, "It's okay to talk to your patients about alternative medicine, and even to suggest they go somewhere else to have it, just not in our facility!"

I was shocked. That was the first time since I began integrating energy work into my medical practice in 1993 that anyone had taken issue with it. Back when I started offering Reiki to my patients in addition to their usual medical care, few in the medical community had even heard of energy medicine. At that time, I had been concerned that my employers might object to what I was doing, but it had *never happened*.

"Good grief, Derwood, you knew I was an integrative medicine doc when you hired me. We even talked about it. Besides, Reiki has become mainstream over the years since I started introducing it to my patients. It's available in the complementary medicine departments of most major medical centers, and Reiki volunteers work with cancer and surgical patients in hundreds of community hospitals. For over a decade, the National Institute of Health has been funding studies to evaluate the effectiveness of various forms of energy healing.

"How on earth could you have decided now, in this time of enlightenment, that my using Reiki as an adjunct to Western medical care could possibly hurt your hospital's reputation?"

It was like talking to a brick wall. When presenting the facts made no difference, I did the only thing that made sense to me. I turned in my resignation.

Clearly, unemployment was not an option. So I called my previous employer, who had frequently phoned to request that I come back to work in his emergency department, and told him that I'd be available in a couple months. There was no doubt in my mind that I had done the right thing by leaving a facility where I was forbidden from practicing the kind of medicine I believed in, but I was more than a little apprehensive about returning to the other hospital.

There were two reasons why I had left that hospital a few months earlier. Location was one issue. It was almost an hour farther away from my home, a drive that frequently became impossible in winter when the mountain roads were closed because of heavy snowfall.

The second reason caused an uncomfortable churning in my gut. That ER saw more violent drunks and drug addicts than any other hospital I had worked in. Taking care of those people was not only unpleasant, it could be downright terrifying. The hospital had no security. The willing assistance of local police was often the only thing that kept my staff and me from harm. I reminded myself of all the nice patients I had treated there, of the staff members I had truly missed in the months I'd been away, and tried not to focus on my anxieties.

Over the next few days, I frequently looked up at the sky and asked, "Okay, Spirit, what's the lesson I'm supposed to learn by returning to that place?"

I was met only with a reflection of my own fears.

Finally, when I was driving to work one morning, Spirit sent the answer.

As always, I said my daily affirmations for a half hour and then turned on my MP3 player so I could sing along for the rest of the two-hour drive. The display read: "There is no information on this unit." After a couple more unsuccessful attempts to get it to work, I started singing on my own.

Without giving it any thought, I began with my favorite chant from Dances of Universal Peace. The words are in Sanskrit and I have to admit that I rarely think about their meaning when I sing them. The melody is beautiful and always brings back so many wonderful memories. Looking back, I realize that while I was enjoying the song, my subconscious was providing the answer to my query. The words to the chant are Metta, Karuna, Mudita, Uppekha. They mean:

Metta: caring, loving kindness displayed to all you meet.
Karuna: compassion or mercy, the special kindness shown to those who suffer.
Mudita: sympathetic joy, being happy for others, without a trace of envy.
Uppekha: equanimity or levelness, the ability to accept others as they are.

After several minutes, I found myself drifting into a different song, one I had not sung in years. It was a part of the Desiderata poem that my dance leader, Grace, had set to music. "You are a child of the Universe, no less than the earth and the stars, you have a right to be here. I am a child of the Universe, no less than the earth and the stars, I have a right to be here. Whether it is clear to me or you, the Universe is unfolding as it should."

When I sang, "You are a child of the Universe," I suddenly saw before me the face of one of the drunken patients from the town I was worried about returning to. As I continued singing to his image, tears flowed down my cheeks and clarity filled my mind. I realized there was a very special purpose for my returning to work there.

If I'm to be the healer I believe myself to be, I may not like how some of my patients act or some of the choices they have made, but I do have to open my heart and respect their souls and to feel COMPASSION. Spirit was sending me back there to learn compassion.

Before beginning my drive home from work the following morning, I decided to try my MP3 one more time, just for the heck of it. It worked perfectly! Clearly I was supposed to sing that song and learn that lesson the day before.

I felt good about my choices and joy on my path.

My heart was open.

*The best and most beautiful things in the world
cannot be seen or even touched.
They must be felt from the heart.
~Helen Keller*

Afterword

It has been an incredible journey, stepping from ordinary reality into the realm of energy healing. In the process I have not only learned about some of the great mysteries the Universe has to offer, but about myself.

All of us who are healers know that healing is like peeling away the layers of an onion. We always have more learning, more healing and more growing to do. But then, isn't that why we are all here on this glorious, challenging, ever-changing planet?

It has been a joy having the opportunity to share some of my journey with you. I wish you healing and peace.

Many paths lead
from the foot of the mountain,
But at the peak
we all gaze at the single bright moon.
~Ikkyu

Part II
Exercises and Meditations

What I have learned after doing healing work for more than two decades is that the intent and belief that drive the process are more important than whatever method I employ on any specific occasion. At the same time, I must acknowledge that mastering specific techniques has often been the means through which I have learned to direct my own abilities. It is in this light that I would like to share some of the exercises and meditations that have helped me gain a better understanding of myself and of the gifts the Universe has brought through me.

I encourage you to view them as steppingstones that will help you to suspend your own disbelief and move forward on your path. I suggest that you focus on the ones that call to you. Let them help you gain an understanding of how you can work with energy and of your own gifts.

*When you believe that something is possible
When you have the basic tools to work with
When you know that
you are the one who must make it happen
You will discover your own method
to accomplish any task.*

You only need to believe.

Playing With Energy

Energy Balls

This exercise is a wonderful way to start playing with energy. It will help you begin to develop your ability to perceive and manipulate energy. It is also a simple self-healing technique that anyone can learn in a few minutes.

Children have a lot of fun with this exercise and will often make a game of it, adding color and texture to their energy balls and even passing them back and forth between each other. But then, they're not inhibited by the limitations that society has taught us to believe to be true.

Sit comfortably in a chair or on the floor in a quiet room.

Close your eyes.

Take several slow, deep breaths.

Rub your palms together several times.

With your palms facing each other, slowly move your hands apart.

Gradually bring your hands back together until they are close to each other but not touching.

Shift your awareness to the space between your hands.

Slowly move your palms farther apart and then close together again, keeping your awareness on the space between them. Repeat this movement three or four times.

What is in that space?

Do you feel heat? Cold? Pressure?

Does it have a density? A color? A texture?

Continue moving your hands apart and back together for several minutes.

As you do so, imagine that you are compressing whatever substance you may be feeling in that space.

Continue shaping and compressing whatever is in the space between your hands until you feel that you have formed it into a dense ball. (The action is like forming a snowball.)

Gently place the ball into whatever part of your body may need healing.

If there is no specific problem area in your body, place the ball of energy into your heart.

The Steel Arm

This is an exercise I teach at the beginning of my first degree Reiki classes and at talks that serve as an introduction to energy medicine. Anyone can do it with just a minute or two of coaching. It helps to instill confidence in the insecure and helps those who don't believe in all this "Woo-Woo stuff" to release their prejudices.

This one takes two people working as a team.

The person who is going to create the steel arm, we'll call her "A" should stand comfortably with her feet a shoulder width apart.

She should raise her dominant arm out to the side so the upper arm is at about a thirty degree angle from her body.

The arm should be slightly flexed at the elbow, with the palm facing upward. It is important that the joint not be locked.

The second person, we'll call her "B", stands at right angles to "A", about eighteen inches away, facing A's extended arm.

Person B's hand on the side closer to person A's body should rest lightly on A's bicep.

B's other hand is placed on the underside of A's forearm.

B should gently attempt to bend A's arm while A resists with her muscles.

Please keep this gentle. We're trying to see what an arm feels like when the muscles are in resistance, and to get an idea of how much pressure it takes to bend it. It's *not* an arm wrestling contest. The goal is for there to be NO injuries.

Now they will repeat the exercise only with a different twist.

They will stand in the same positions they were in for the first part of the exercise.

"A" will close her eyes and take a moment to relax her body, then she will take several slow, deep breaths.

Each time she exhales, she will imagine that she is breathing rigid steel down her extended arm and out through the tips of her fingers.

After several breathes, when she can imagine that her arm is filled with steel, she will keep her arm muscles totally relaxed and nod her head.

"B" will then try to gently bend the arm while "A" keeps her muscles relaxed and continues breathing steel through her extended arm.

Feel the difference?

Now, reverse positions so that "B" becomes the person with the extended arm and "A" tries to bend her arm.

Do both parts of the exercise.

Spoon Bending

More than a party trick, spoon bending is a first step toward developing your psychokinetic abilities.

You will not be able to return the utensils to their original shape after this exercise, so don't use your good silverware. Choose a collection of inexpensive spoons and forks. (Second hand stores are a great source of inexpensive tableware.)

***Do not use knives for this exercise.
They may shatter.***

Sit in a comfortable chair or on the floor.

Using the thumb and first two fingers of your dominant hand, hold a spoon at the narrow spot of the handle, just below the bowl.

Take several slow, deep breaths.

With each breath imagine that you are inhaling white light.

Feel the light collect in your head.

After the third breath, exhale the white light in a quick puff.

Feel the light move from your head, down your arm and out through the tips of your fingers into the spoon.

Relax your spine until it begins to curve forward in a gentle arc.

Imagine that the stem of the spoon is softening and bending as your spine is relaxing and bending.

Gently grasp one end of the spoon in each hand and bend or twist the spoon.

The metal should be soft and pliant for a few seconds.

As you bend the handle of the spoon, you are releasing energy from the bonds in the metal so it will become quite warm.

After a few seconds, the metal will become rigid again.

You must learn a new way to think
Before you can master a new way to be.
~Marianne Williamson

Clearing and Protection

Energy is contagious. When we're in a room full of happy people, we begin to feel some of the joy that has permeated the room. Conversely, when confronted with someone who is angry or distressed, we often take on those emotions and begin to feel anxious or even downright angry ourselves.

In order to be able to work in an environment where strong emotions are the norm, or for that matter, to simply be able to walk peacefully in the world and remain unscathed by the emotions of those who surround me, I have adopted the practice of placing an energetic shield around myself each morning before I leave my home. When confronted by a difficult situation, I frequently take a few deep breaths and, at the same time, visualize my shield firmly in place. The act of visualizing the shield serves to reinforce it.

Before they begin doing any kind of energy work on each other, I always teach my students to clear and protect themselves. The process is quite simple.

It actually consists of two exercises. The first is for clearing, the second creates a protective shield.

Begin by following these steps to clear yourself of any negative thoughts, feelings or emotions that you may be carrying.

Clearing Yourself

When you are learning to do this exercise, it's easier if you create a little distance between yourself and any surrounding objects or people. Once you get the hang of it, you can do it just as effectively when you are sitting at a desk or even standing in a crowd.

If possible, stand at least a couple feet from any other person, furniture or plants.

Straighten your spine and relax your arms and shoulders.

Take a slow, deep breath.

Keep your shoulders relaxed and use your diaphragm to draw in the air. (If you are doing this correctly your abdomen will protrude when you are inhaling but your chest will not move very much.)

As you inhale, imagine that you are drawing a beam of golden or white light in through the top of your head.

See and feel the white light flow through your head, your neck, your shoulders and your chest.

As the white light comes into your abdomen begin to exhale.

On the exhale, imagine that your breath is pushing the light around your spine and down through your abdomen, your pelvis, your hips, your thighs, your knees, your calves and finally out through the soles of your feet and into the earth.

Imagine that the white light is cleansing your body of any negative emotions as it passes through.

Repeat the cleansing breath three times.

I not only use this exercise as a prelude to shielding myself, I use it to clear and center myself whenever I feel stressed or out of balance. No matter how busy I am, no matter how chaotic my surroundings, I always have time to take a couple slow, deep breaths.

Even if your life is too hectic to spend long periods of time in meditation, you always have time to breathe. I recommend that you get into the habit of taking a few cleansing breaths at the start of each hour. You can do it while you're sitting at your desk. You can even do it when you're out walking in a crowed mall or in the middle of a tense meeting at work. No one will be the wiser and you will feel a whole lot better and be much more able to cope with whatever is happening around you.

Shielding

When you feel clear and relaxed, it's time to create your protective shield. Think of it as a small version of the force field they put around the spaceships on Star Trek. They don't want the bad guys to be able to shoot them with laser beams, but they do want to be able to send and receive messages from the good guys.

You do NOT want to be encased in impenetrable armor. You want all the good things: love, friendship, healing and joy—to freely enter your space. You also want to be able to send all those good things back out to others.

At the same time, you want to be protected from taking on someone else's negative emotions: fear, anger, sadness—and you want them to be safe from receiving those same feelings from you.

In order to do this, you will set rules for your shield. You must decide what is allowed to pass freely in and out and what is not. Then you will use affirmations to set those rules firmly in your own mind and into the energetic structure of your shield.

Imagine that your body is surrounded by a shimmering, silver bubble.

Visualize that bubble.

It is spherical.

It sits about two or three feet from your body in all directions.

Now it's time to set the rules for your shield. Remember that you want it to keep bad things away from you, but you don't want those bad things to bounce off your shield and hurt someone else. You want them to dissipate into the atmosphere, to become harmless.

You do not want your shield to be so strong that nothing can get in or out. It should let good things cross freely.

Set the rules of your shield with an affirmation. You can say it out loud, or repeat it silently to yourself.

The affirmation I say when I create my own shield is:

"I am surrounded by a silver protective shield that dissipates all negativity and harm. It is a sanctuary of love, friendship, healing, support, joy, laughter, wisdom, passion and learning. It is freely permeable to the Reiki

and to all loving and healing forces of the Universe and the planet, protective of my vital life source energy (my soul) and open and welcoming to my loving spirit teachers and guides."

Your own affirmation will vary from mine, depending on your personal needs and beliefs.

When I finish creating my own shield each morning, I also visualize a protective bubble around each of my pets, my home and my car.

Creating a Sacred Space

The traditions of most ancient cultures include a variety of rituals for cleansing and purifying the environment. Some people believe that power comes from the ceremony itself, others believe that the power comes solely from the intent and belief of the person performing the ceremony.

My personal spiritual beliefs have roots in Celtic, Native American and Buddhist traditions. The cleansing rituals that have power for me stem from those traditions.

Smudging

When I move into a new house, prepare my home for a special event, or simply wish to cleanse a space of any negative energies or emotions, the first thing I do is a smudging ceremony.

Smudging is a Native American practice that calls upon the spirit of sage or cedar to clear an environment of negative energy. As with any ritual, the intent and belief of the practitioner are the driving forces of the process.

When I smudge my home, I usually play Native American flute music. The music helps put me into the correct frame of mind to perform the ceremony, though it is certainly not necessary.

It's a good idea to turn off any smoke detectors in the house before performing this ritual.

Open a door or window so negative energy has a route to leave the space.

Hold a bunch of white sage that has been bound together into a smudge stick or you may choose to fill a fire-resistant dish or bowl with loose leaves of dried white sage.

Light the sage leaves. (I use a long ended butane fire starter.)

When all the leaves have started to burn, blow out the flames so they are left smoldering and smoking.

Walk slowly through each room allowing the smoke to fill the room.

Forcefully call out, "Spirit of the sage, Great Spirit (Father, Mother, God) I ask that you help me to cleanse this room, this house and myself of all negative energies and entities. Banish from this space all that is not of love and of light. Create a joyful and loving

sanctuary for living, for learning, for healing, for... (Choose your own words here. Your choice will vary according to what is about to take place in the room.)

End with, "I thank you Great Spirit." (Father, Mother, God)

Repeat the process in each room and in the hallways between them.

After smudging inside the house, go outside and walk around the property, smudging and clearing the energy of the land.

Cleansing a Room with Reiki

This is a lovely and simple way to cleanse a room and create an energy vortex. It can be done by anyone who is a Reiki II practitioner or higher.

Begin by taking three slow, deep breaths.

As you inhale, draw white light in through the top of your head.

As you exhale, move the light through your body to clear yourself.

Choose a direction to begin with and face that wall.

Draw the Emotional Healing Symbol in the air in front of yourself while repeating its true name three times.

Use your hands, your breath and your intent to drive that symbol into the wall in front of you and into the adjacent corners.

Turn 90 degrees clockwise and repeat the process on the next wall.

Repeat the process until you have sent the symbol into all four walls and are once again facing the wall you started with.

When you are facing that wall, look up and send the emotional symbol into the ceiling above your head while repeating its name three times.

Bring your hands together in prayer position and say, "May this room be cleared of all negative energies."

Next, draw the Distance Symbol in the air in front of yourself while repeating its true name three times.

Use your hands, your breath and your intent to drive the symbol into the wall in front of you and into the corners adjacent to it.

Turn ninety degrees clockwise and repeat the process in the next wall.

Repeat the process until you have sent the symbol into all four walls and are once again facing the wall you started with.

When you are facing that wall, look up and send the Distance Symbol into the ceiling above your head while repeating its name three times.

Bring your hands together in prayer position and say, "May the healings in this room transcend time and place."

Finally, draw the Power Symbol into the air in front of yourself while repeating its true name three times.

With your hands, your breath and your intent, guide the symbol into the wall in front of you and the adjacent corners.

Turn ninety degrees clockwise and repeat the process in the next wall.

Repeat the process until you have sent the symbol into all four walls and are once again facing the wall you started with.

When you are facing that wall, look up and send the Power Symbol into the ceiling above your head while repeating its name three times.

Reach up with your hands and draw down the energy to create a vortex of Reiki energy.

Bring your hands together in prayer position and say, "May this room be filled with the Reiki light."

As a Reiki master, I add one final step. I draw the Master Symbol in the air in front of me and entreat: "May the Goddess be with me."

Creating a Medicine Wheel

Originally a Native American tradition, creating a medicine wheel is not unlike the Celtic practice of casting a circle of stones or salt. All these practices are intended to create a safe environment within a boundary that has been set to block the intrusion of negative energy. In many cases, the rituals are also meant to open an energy vortex of healing and power within the circle.

I have created medicine wheels to encompass each of the major rooms in my home. When I go through my cleansing rituals before a class, or when I prepare for a special occasion, I repeat the ceremony I am about to describe in order to re-establish and reinforce the boundaries of my sacred space and to strengthen the energy vortex I have opened.

Begin by setting your intent. "I wish to create a sacred space for healing."

Prepare the location with a physical cleaning and a ritual of purification such as a smudging ceremony.

Establish the four directions: North, South, East and West.

(When indoors, simply use the directions of the four walls of your room.)

Decide where the boundaries of your sacred space, your Medicine Wheel, will be. (Your medicine wheel may be just large enough for you to sit in— a place where you can go to meditate and to heal— or it may encompass your entire living space.)

Place a stone or crystal at the locations on the boundary of your medicine wheel that correspond to each of the four directions (or at the center of each of the four walls in your room).

Choose any type of stone or crystal that feels "right" to you. (I generally choose rose quartz or smoky quartz. Just follow your intuition and you will make the right choice.)

Energize your stones:

Beginning in the South, approach and face the stone. Inhale deeply. As you inhale, draw

Universal energy through your crown chakra and let it flow into your center.

As you exhale, beam the energy from your third eye, your solar plexus and your hands into the stone. (Reiki practitioners may also beam the Power Symbol from their hands at this time.)

Continue the process until you can see a change in the stone and you know that it is "full".

When you know you are done, turn to the West.

(Indoors, turn in a clockwise direction to face the adjacent wall)

Proceed around the circle, stopping to energize each stone. When you have charged the last stone, return to face the stone in the South (the wall where you began).

Once all four stones have been charged with energy, you need to connect them.

Stand in the center of the space.

Using your mind and your hands, reach up and draw a ribbon of healing energy from the Universe into the room and connect it to the first stone. Connect each of the remaining stones to a similar energy ribbon.

Next, draw an energy ribbon from one stone to the next as you move clockwise around the circle.

SEE the energy connection forming between the stones as you direct your energy ribbon. You are shaping an enclosed column of light whose boundaries are defined by the placement of the stones.

While performing the final step say, "Great Spirit (Father, Mother, God), I ask that you help me to connect these stones, to create a vortex of healing. Banish all negative energies and entities from this space. Create a space where only that which is of love and light may exist. I thank you, Great Spirit."

When you have finished, stand inside your medicine wheel.

Take a moment to face each stone and give honor to that direction.

Thank the spirits respectfully before taking your leave.

You have just opened a vortex of healing and purification, a sacred space in which negative energy cannot exist.

Sometimes your only available transportation
Is a leap of faith
~Margaret Shepard

Connecting With the Earth

Over the years, a number of very simple practices that help me to re-connect with earth energy and recharge myself have become part of my daily life. They can be done in a few minutes or can carry on for hours, whatever your needs and your lifestyle allow.

Walking

In Ayurveda it is believed that energy enters the left side of the body and is released from the right side of the body. Using that simple principle, I am able to turn any outdoor walk, whether I am hiking in the desert or simply walking to the end of the driveway to collect my mail, into a healing experience with just a few simple steps. Literally.

Start walking.

As your left foot comes into contact with the ground, begin to inhale slowly.

Continue inhaling to the count of three while your weight is primarily on your left foot.

As you inhale, imagine that you are drawing the green, healing energies of the planet in through the sole of your left foot.

Feel that energy moving up your leg and swirling through your body.

When your right foot comes into contact with the ground, begin to exhale.

Continue exhaling to the count of three while your weight is resting primarily on your right foot.

As you exhale, imagine that the green energy that has been swirling through your body is now moving into your right leg, down to your foot and out through the sole of your right foot back into the earth.

Repeat the cycle with each step.

Eventually, you will be able to move earth energy through your body whenever you walk with almost no conscious effort.

Sharing Energy With a Tree

This old Qi Gong exercise is one of my favorite healing practices.

When you are outside, position yourself a few feet from the base (trunk) of your favorite bush, tree or cactus.

Face the plant.

Stand erect with your feet a shoulder's width apart.

Relax your shoulders.

Allow your knees to bend slightly, so they are not locked.

Feel your feet planted firmly on the ground.

Take a slow, deep breath.

As you inhale, imagine that you are drawing white healing energy from the Universe in through the top of your head.

Feel that energy flow through your head, your neck, your shoulders, your spine, your chest, your abdomen, your hips and your legs until it reaches the soles of your feet.

As you begin to exhale, imagine that you are pushing the energy from the soles of your feet, through the ground into the roots of the plant.

See the energy move through the roots, up the trunk of your tree, out to the tips of its branches where it will be released back into the Universe.

With the next breath, reverse the process.

Imagine that as you inhale, you are drawing white light in through the branches of the tree.

See it move through the branches, into the trunk, out through the roots and finally from the tip of the roots, through the ground into the soles of your own feet.

As you begin to exhale, see and feel the energy that has come through the tree move from your feet, up your legs to your thighs, hips, pelvis, abdomen, chest and finally up your neck, through your head and out through the top of your head to be released back into the Universe.

Repeat the steps until you feel that both you and the tree have been replenished.

One morning, on the way home from work, I was driving on a long, lonely road through a magnificent area of Sonoran desert, longing to lay down by one of the sahuaros to soak up its energy. I suddenly realized that I could connect with the cactus even if I couldn't stop the car, get through the fence and lay down on the earth.

I started doing a modified version of the energy sharing exercise. When I inhaled, I visualized energy flowing into the top of the sahuaro, moving through it and into the ground. I drew in energy from the sahuaro and the earth in through the soles of my feet (and the floor of the car.) It flowed through my body to the top of my head. When I exhaled, I sent energy back into the Universe. With the next indrawn breath, I pulled Universal energy in through the top of my head, through my body and then, on the exhale, into the ground and back through the sahuaro. I found it worked best when I focused on a plant a good distance away so that I could get through an entire breathing cycle before passing it.

It was a fabulous way to recharge after a grueling twenty-four hour shift in a busy ER, but I have to caution, **DO NOT attempt to do this if you are driving on a road where there are other cars around you.**

Opening Your Heart to the Earth

This was one of my favorite daily rituals when I lived on the ranch in the Sonoran desert, but all you really need is a clean patch of earth large enough to lay down on in any location where you feel safe.

Place a light blanket or jacket down on the ground. (You can skip this step if you don't feel you need it.)

Lay face down on the earth. Cradle your head on your arms and shift your legs until you are in a comfortable position.

Relax.

Take a slow, deep breath.

As you inhale, imagine that you are inhaling the green healing energies of the earth in through your heart.

When you exhale, imagine that you are sending love from your heart back into the earth.

Keep breathing in and out through your heart until you feel your heart is full.

When you are done, you should feel calm and rejuvenated.

Connecting With People: Create Your Own Prayer Chain or Healing Chain

This is really very similar to the telephone trees that people have created for years.

When you or a loved one has a serious injury or medical problem, send an E-mail to friends. The E-mail should contain a little information about the person who requires healing including the person's name, what city and state they are in (or what hospital) and a brief description of their condition. It is helpful to include a photograph of the person since many people find it easier to send distance healing if they can focus on a visual image of the recipient.

Ask the everyone to send prayers and/or healing energy and request that they forward your e-mail to any other healing chains or prayer circles they participate in.

If the request is for someone other than your self or your own child or pet, ask for that person's consent before sending out her name or photograph.

This is also a lovely way to coordinate a group prayer or healing to send to a population or a situation on the planet.

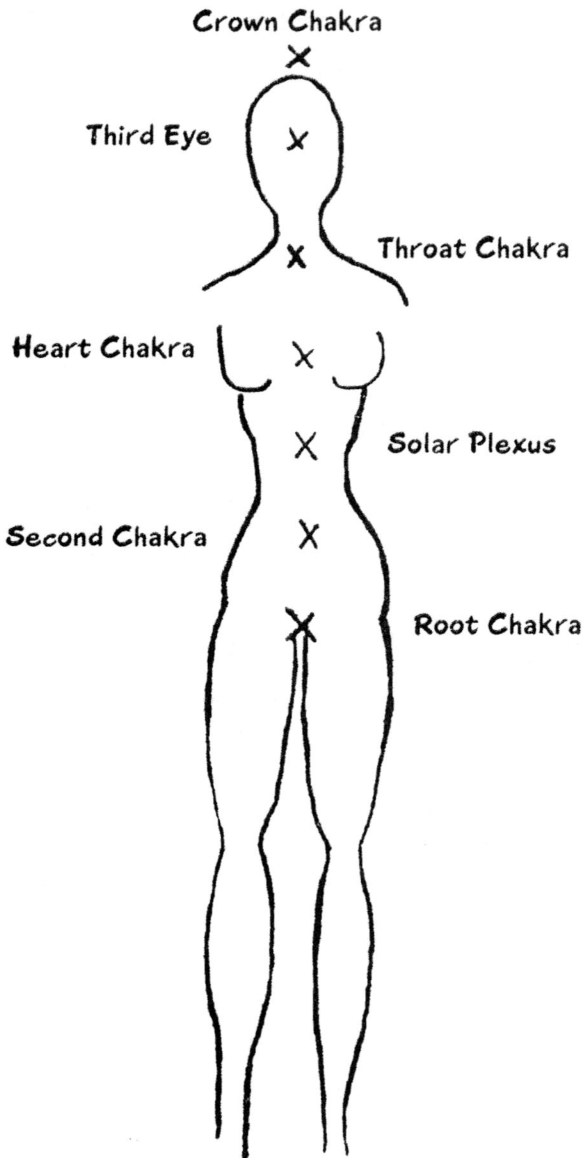

Crown Chakra
Third Eye
Throat Chakra
Heart Chakra
Solar Plexus
Second Chakra
Root Chakra

Chakras

Chakras are the primary energy centers of the body. Each has a specific location, and color. Specific emotions and feelings are tied to each chakra and its associated organs.

The first chakra is just below the junction of the thighs. Its color is red. It is associated with feelings of survival. It connects us to the earth and to society.

The second chakra is in the lower abdomen, just below the navel. Its color is orange. It relates to sexuality, self-esteem and also to the ability to move forward. Organs associated with it include the sexual organs, the intestines, the kidneys and the hips.

The third chakra is at the Solar Plexus. It is yellow. It is a center of power and the opposite of power, which is fear. Organs associated with it include the liver, spleen and stomach.

The fourth is the Heart Chakra, in the center

of the chest. It is green. It is the place of love and, the opposite of love, anger. Organs associated with it include the heart and lungs.

The Throat Chakra is number five. It is sky blue. It gives one the confidence to express oneself. It is also the connection between the primal centers of the lower body and the higher centers of thought and spirituality. It is associated with the thyroid and parathyroid glands.

The sixth chakra or Third Eye is in the center of the forehead, just above the juncture of the eyebrows. It is deep, amethyst purple. It is a place of insight. It is associated with the pineal gland and pituitary gland.

The seventh or Crown Chakra is our connection with Spirit. It gleams golden and is at the top of the head.

Opening Your Chakras

Each evening, before going to sleep, I like to do this simple exercise to open my chakras and clear my energy field. I give myself Reiki while doing the exercise, but I have taught it to people who have no other training in energy healing and they still find it to be a very effective tool.

Lay in a comfortable position either on the floor or on a bed.

Place both hands lightly over your first chakra.

Take a slow, deep breath.

Imagine that you are inhaling red light through the top of your head.

Visualize it moving through your head, your neck, your chest, your abdomen and pelvis until it comes to rest in your first chakra.

Exhale the red light out through the front of your first chakra.

Take another slow, deep breath.

Imagine that you are inhaling red light up through the soles of your feel.

Visualize it moving up through your legs until it comes to rest in your first chakra.

Exhale the red light out through the front of your first chakra.

Repeat the process until you have drawn light in through the top of your head and through the soles of your feet three times each.

When you are a little more experienced at breathing energy through your body, you will be able to inhale light from the top of your head and the soles of your feet at the same time and then exhale it all from your chakra in a single breath.

> Leave your left hand over your first chakra and place your right hand on your second chakra.
>
> Take a slow, deep breath.
>
> Imagine that you are inhaling orange light in through the top of your head.
>
> Visualize it moving through your head, your neck, your chest and your abdomen until it comes to rest in your second chakra.
>
> Exhale the orange light out through the front of your second chakra.
>
> Take another slow, deep breath.
>
> Imagine that you are inhaling orange light up through the soles of your feet.
>
> Visualize it moving up through your legs and pelvis until it comes to rest in your second chakra.
>
> Exhale the orange light out through the front of your second chakra.
>
> Repeat the process until you have drawn light in through the top of your head and through the soles of your feet three times each.

Leave your right hand on your second chakra and place your left hand on your solar plexus.

Take a slow, deep breath.

Imagine that you are inhaling yellow light in through the top of your head.

Visualize it moving through your head, your neck and your chest and then into your solar plexus.

Exhale the yellow light out through the front of your solar plexus.

Take another slow, deep breath.

Imagine that you are inhaling yellow light up through the soles of your feet.

Visualize it moving up through your legs, pelvis and abdomen until it comes to rest in your solar plexus.

Exhale the yellow light out through the front of your solar plexus.

Repeat the process until you have drawn light in through the top of your head and through the soles of your feet three times each.

Leave your left hand over your solar plexus and place your right hand on your heart chakra.

Take a slow, deep breath.

Imagine that you are inhaling green light in through the top of your head.

Visualize it moving through your head and your neck and finally coming to rest in your heart.

Exhale the green light out through the front of your heart chakra.

Take another slow, deep breath.

Imagine that you are inhaling green light up through the soles of your feet.

Visualize it moving up through your legs, your pelvis and your abdomen until it comes to rest in your heart chakra.

Exhale the green light out through the front of your heart chakra.

Repeat the process until you have drawn light in through the top of your head and through the soles of your feet three times each.

Leave your right hand over your heart chakra and place your left hand on your throat chakra.

Take a slow, deep breath.

Imagine that you are inhaling sky blue light

in through the top of your head.

Visualize it moving through your head and coming to rest in your throat.

Exhale the blue light out through the front of your throat chakra.

Take another slow, deep breath.

Imagine that you are inhaling sky blue light up through the soles of your feet.

Visualize it moving through your feet and ankles, your legs and thighs, your hips and pelvis, your abdomen, your chest and shoulders and finally coming to rest in your neck.

Exhale the blue light out through the front of your throat chakra.

Repeat the process until you have drawn light in through the top of your head and through the soles of your feet three times each.

Leave your left hand over your throat chakra and place your right hand over your third eye.

Take a slow, deep breath.

Imagine that you are inhaling deep amethyst purple light in through the top of your head.

Visualize it coming to rest in your third eye.

Exhale the purple light out through the front of your third eye.

Take another slow, deep breath.

Imagine that you are inhaling amethyst light up through the soles of your feet.

Visualize it moving up through your legs, your pelvis, your abdomen, your chest, your neck and head until it comes to rest in your third eye.

Exhale the purple light out through your third eye.

Repeat the process until you have drawn light in through the top of your head and through the soles of your feet three times each.

Leave your hands where they are or move them to any place where they are most comfortable.

Take a slow, deep breath.

Imagine that you are inhaling white light in through the souls of your feet.

Visualize it moving through your ankles and legs, your thighs, your hips and pelvis, your abdomen and chest, your neck, swirling through your head and finally leaving through the top of your head.

Repeat this process three or more times, until it feels like you are perfectly clear and the energy is moving freely and easily.

Take another slow deep breath. This time imagine that you are drawing white light in through the top of your head. Use your breath to move the white light through your head and neck, your shoulders, your chest and abdomen, your pelvis, your hips and thighs, your knees and lower legs, your ankles and finally out through the soles of your feet. Repeat this process several times.

Close your eyes and enjoy a peaceful night's sleep.

God sleeps in rocks
Dreams in plants
Stirs in animals
And awakens in man
~ Sufi saying

A Journey Into Creativity

The roots of this exercise come from the ancient Celtic belief that we live many lifetimes, not only in human form but as animals, plants or even as the wind in the trees. I was first introduced to the exercise at a shamanic journeying workshop. I love the history behind the exercise as much as the creativity it inspires.

I have developed a simpler version that is equally inspiring but much more accessible. I first introduced it as a guided meditation in my Reiki master classes, but have since presented it at large workshops with much more diverse groups of students. The results were equally exciting.

This exercise also works well for children. A friend of mine who teaches fifth grade used it with her class. Everyone in that group, as in all the others, effortlessly created something beautiful.

This exercise is a little labor intensive to prepare for, but worth the effort. While best suited for a group, you can do it on your own. If you are going to try it solo, I would recommend recording the instructions below and doing it as a guided meditation, so that you can fully immerse yourself in the process.

Preparation

This is the labor-intensive part, but once it's done, it's done forever. You need to create a set of cards. I use four different colors of three by five inch index cards. Ideally you should have at least twenty of each color. *(You can purchase a singe pack of about 60 or 100 index cards that contains equal numbers of cards in each of four different colors.)*

Print the name of a different kind of plant on each card of the first color. Choose common names that anyone will recognize. Examples might include: Rose, Daisy, Maple tree, Cactus, Fern, Pine tree. Be as specific as you think the people you intend to share the exercise with will be able to identify. This will vary depending on the part of the country you live in and the age of the intended participants.

Color number two is for animals. This one's easy: dog, cat, mouse, rabbit, lizard, snake, elephant, zebra, lion, tiger, cricket, mosquito, spider, clam, starfish, shark, whale, dolphin, humming bird, eagle etc.

Color number three is for seasons and weather phenomena: summer, winter, autumn, spring, snow, rain, thunder, lightning, wind, monsoon, tornado, hurricane, blizzard. You get the idea.

The fourth set is for places in nature: rock, mountain, cliff, river, ocean, stream, desert, prairie, forest. If you can't come up with enough variations, it's okay to repeat some on more than one card.

Now comes the fun part.

Keep each group of cards in a separate pile.

Shuffle each pile of cards.

With the cards face down, ask the participants to pick one card from each of the four sets.

Allow them a minute to read the cards so they will recall what is on them.

Everyone should have a blank sheet of paper and a pen or pencil.

Have them write the words I AM at the beginning of the first line.

Play some kind of music that does not have any lyrics. My favorite for this exercise is Karma Moffett's CD *Golden Bowls*. It's an exquisite symphony of Tibetan bowls. The sound from each bowl is keyed to a specific chakra, so playing it during the exercise will encourage participants to react to the experience with their whole body and through all their senses.

Other music that lends itself well to this exercise includes Native American flute or any soft, new age music. My friend chose classical music for her fifth graders. Mozart and Debussy would be good choices, but anything that moves you will work.

I was introduced to a similar process as a shamanic journey, so the only sounds that day were the beat of drums and the voice of the group leader.

While it may not be essential, I find that the right music helps people to step out of their logical minds.

Finally, you're ready to start.

Have the participants sit or lie in a comfortable position.

Read the following guided meditation aloud in a soft, slow voice.

OR

Record the words in advance and play them back to guide everyone through the exercise.

(Allow at least 10 or fifteen seconds of silence after each line, so the participants can fully experience the feelings and images that are being evoked by the words.)

Close your eyes.

Take a slow, deep breath.

As you exhale, allow yourself to release any tension or worries you may be carrying.

Take several more slow, deep breaths.

Feel yourself relax more completely with each breath.

Take another slow, deep breath.

Now, imagine that you are your plant.

Where are you?

What is happening around you?

What do you look like?

What do you feel?

What do you hear?

What do you see?

What do you smell?

Do you make any sound?

(Allow a minute or two of silence)

Take another slow, deep breath.

Now, imagine that you are your animal.

Where are you?

What is happening around you?

What do you look like?

What do you feel?

What do you hear?

What do you see?

What do you smell?

Do you make any sound?

(Allow a minute or two of silence.)

Take another slow, deep breath.

Now, imagine that you are your season.

Where are you?

What is happening around you?

What do you look like?

What do you feel?

What do you hear?

What do you see?

What do you smell?

Do you make any sound?

(Allow a minute or two of silence)

Take another slow, deep breath.

Now, imagine that you are your place.

Where are you?

What is happening around you?

What do you look like?

What do you feel?

What do you hear?

What do you see?

What do you smell?

Do you make any sound?

(Allow a minute or two of silence.)

Instruct your participants to open their eyes (and sit up if they are lying down).

Tell them to remain completely silent as they pick up their pen and paper and write down what they experienced during the exercise.

Each line must start with the words I AM. There are no other directions

Allow them ten or fifteen minutes of silence to write. (For young children allow only about five minutes.) If everyone has put down their pencil sooner than the time you had anticipated, go ahead and call time.

It's fun to allow people to read what they have written out loud if they feel comfortable doing so.

Each of the exercises I have shared with you has brought its own special richness to my life. I hope that you will also find them to be a source of healing and growth.

Namaste.

Glossary

Ascites: free fluid in the abdominal cavity

Fibroid: benign tumor of the uterine muscle

Lymphatics: the channels that carry excess tissue fluid back into the general circulation

Lymphedema: Swelling in a limb that results from blocked lymphatic channels

Namaste: the goddess in me salutes the god or goddess in you

Ortho-phobic: fear of dealing with orthopedic procedures

Orthopod: medical slang for an orthopedic surgeon

Stifle: the joint between the thigh bone and the lower leg bones in the hind leg of a horse; equivalent to the knee joint in humans. In horses, the term "knee" refers to a joint in the front leg.

Resources

Healing Instruments
www.ichingsystems.net

To learn more about Spoon Bending Parties
http://www.jackhouck.com

About the Author

Jeri Mills is a physician, veterinarian, Reiki master teacher, intuitive healer, writer and storyteller.

Her articles on women's health and integrative medicine have appeared in newspapers and journals in the United States, Canada, France and the UK. She has lectured internationally about the integration of Western medicine and Energy medicine.

Her purpose is to serve as a bridge between Eastern and Western medicine. Her passion is to bring healing to all she touches.

Visit her on the WEB at
www.JeriMillsMD.com